BANKER OCCUPATION
Waging Financial War on Humanity

BANKER OCCUPATION

Waging Financial War on Humanity

by

STEPHEN LENDMAN

CLEAR DAY BOOKS

ISBN: 978-0-9845255-8-4
E-book: 978-0-9845255-9-1

In-house editor: Diana G. Collier
Cover: R. Jordan P. Santos
Charging Bull image based on the photo "Charging Bull
by Sebastian Alvarez (http://www.flickr.com/photos/
aseba/6179708990/in/set-72157627744672130/)

Clear Day Books
A division of
Clarity Press, Inc.
Ste. 469, 3277 Roswell Rd. NE
Atlanta, GA. 30305 , USA
http://www.claritypress.com

Today financial war rages.
Stopping it depends on putting money power back
in public hands where it belongs.

This book is dedicated to people in the struggle to achieve it.

Table of Contents

1

WALL STREET RUNS AMERICA

Major Wall Street banks occupy and control Washington. I wrote about it at length in my earlier book, *How Wall Street Fleeces America*.[1]Their officials recycle from banking to government and back again, making policy, and enforcing it with their money power supremacy to achieve virtually everything they want.

Political Washington salutes and obeys. Money power in private hands and democracy can't co-exist. It buys what it wants at the expense of government of, by and for the people—the kind of government that in actuality never existed and doesn't now.

Wall Street crooks have transformed America into an unprecedented money making racket. Facilitated by federal, state and local governments, they make money the old fashioned way. They steal it. Ordinary Americans get scammed. They've lost savings, jobs, homes and futures to let privileged elites get richer and more powerful.

Banking giants controlthe creation and circulation of money, issuing credit and debt for private enrichment. They bribe politicians to pass business friendly laws and turn a blind eye to massive fraud and abuse. It pays off. The banksters got decades of deregulation, outsourcing, economic financialization, and casino capitalist excess. In return, America and Western economies got asset bubbles, record budget and national debt levels, depression-sized unemployment, public deprivation and anger.

Today's crisis is global; the contagion has caused billions to suffer. The economies of entire countries are being wrecked to save the banks. Washington is Wall Street-occupied territory. So are European financial capitals because governments provide trillions of dollars to socialize losses, privatize profits, and hang ordinary people out to dry.

Stopping them depends on putting money power—the creation of money and access to credit—back in public hands where it belongs. There's no other way., When Congress passed the Federal Reserve Act on December 23, 1913, it violated Article 1, Section 8 of the Constitution, giving Congress sole power to coin (create) money and regulate the value thereof.Abolishing or nationalizing the Fed and giving money power back to the people through Congress is step one to regain the rights that have been lost to banker controlled government.

That's Issue Number One that Occupy Wall Street[2] protesters and others spreading across America in dozens of cities must address.

Occupy Together[3] is an "unofficial hub" for burgeoning initiatives heading everywhere "in solidarity with Occupy Wall St."

As word spreads, hidden anger surfaces. Small numbers of protesters grow. So does commitment to stay the course. Activists and ordinary people know something's wrong and they want it changed. The key is understanding that money power is in private hands, and not the hands of the government. Change depends on ending this system that is destroying the future for working Americans.

Major Wall Street firms comprise an illegal private banking cartel monopoly controlling the nation's money, price, supply and availability. For a century, it has looted America's economy for its own self-interest. It's run by unelected, unaccountable crooks in league with corrupt politicians, who are taking bribes in the form of campaign contributions to go along with whatever laws, regulations and policies the bankers want.

Behind closed doors, JP Morgan Chase, Goldman Sachs, Bank of America, Wells Fargo, and other giants run America. They do it by waging financial war on the public.In theory, the Fed was established to stabilize the economy, smooth out the business cycle, manage healthy, sustainable growth, and maintain stable prices.Instead, it has caused multiple recessions, the Great Depression, and today's Greatest Global one. It is responsible for monetary inflation and America's declining standard of living, notably in recent decades.

In fact, a 1913 dollar today isn't worth a plug nickel, and given reckless Greenspan/Bernanke money creation the dollar's value is eroding entirely. Notably the Fed caused:

- rising consumer debt;

- record budget and trade deficits;

- a soaring national debt equaling GDP and heading higher;

- escalating personal and business bankruptcies, both up around 35% in 2009 with near record levels persisting in 2010;

- millions of home foreclosures in America's worst ever housing Depression;

- unemployment at nearly 23%;

- loss of the nation's manufacturing base;

- shocking levels of poverty in the world's richest country;

- an unprecedented wealth gap; and

- a hugely unstable economy lurching from one crisis to another.

The Fed lets money power in private hands profit hugely by swindling investors, buying valued assets cheap, consolidating to greater size. The Fed gives it an open checkbook access to trillions for speculation and big bonuses.

Easy money, market manipulation, deregulation, reckless speculation, counterproductive fixes, and unsustainable debt caused today's crisis.

Why else would gold and silver prices soar? Bad policy assures worse trouble ahead. Instead of the excesses bing washed out, they increase over time. Eventually, an unsustainable house of cards collapses, especially when credit contraction persists. The combination of monopoly money power in private hands combined with financialization at the expense of industrial America produced policies that are wrecking the country and futures of ordinary workers.

Job creation is moribund. Industrial America keeps imploding. High-paying jobs are exported. Workers are exploited for greater profits, and no one's acting to revive stable, sustainable long-term growth.

America's FIRE sector (finance, insurance, and real estate) fueled casino capitalist speculation rather than investment in capital goods—in plant, equipment, transportation, and public utilities that fueled earlier business cycle expansions. Instead of making better things for better living, America's financialized economy proliferates unbridled greed, fueled by limitless amounts of privately created money.

Since the 1970s, wages stagnated and lost purchasing power. Inflation rose. Benefits like retirement savings eroded. Household debt rose to compensate. Now it takes two wage-earners to keep up with what was earned by one, years back.

Accumulating enormous excesses, monopoly money power

caused 2008's global collapse. Capitalism's dark side and destructive contradictions were exposed, particularly its financialized form.

Money power in private hands is exploitively destructive. Global populations are harmed. As a result, poverty in developed countries soared. In underdeveloped ones it deepened, leaving millions facing destitution and human misery, even death.

Money power buys influence. Wall Street rules America and the world. Deregulated excess produced unprecedented fraud and grand theft, insider trading, misrepresentation, Ponzi schemes, false accounting, market manipulation, toxic financial products, unprecedented profits, and massive public deception.

Deregulation facilitated it. Whatever Wall Street wants it gets. Without money power, Washington can't or won't intercede enough to matter. Trying produces days like 2010's May 6 "flash crash," cratering the Dow 1,000 points, then recovering losses in minutes. Wall Street's power creates or destroys financial assets with keystroke ease.

If Congress had money power and regulatory backbone, too-big-to-fail banks wouldn't exist. Public banks would operate with small private ones. Every state would prosper like North Dakota—the only one with a state-owned bank.

During the height of 2008's financial crisis, North Dakota had its largest ever surplus. Global contagion cratered other states. If they operated like North Dakota, prosperity would replace gloom.

If federal, state or local governments lend their own money, profit isn't at issue so rates can be low and affordable to businesses, farmers, and private individuals. Moreover, for federal, state, and municipality needs, government-issued credit is interest-free.

In addition, public banks don't have to earn profits. They're not beholden to Wall Street or shareholders. Only federal, state or local community creditworthiness matters.

In over 235 years, neither America nor any state went bankrupt. Only poorly governed Arkansas defaulted during the Great Depression. Under publicly run banks, sustained prosperity is possible, inflation free, *as long as recycled money goes for productive economic growth.*

Whenever this was tried, it worked impressively, including in colonial America for a generation, and today in North Dakota. Why not try it everywhere across America including Washington?

Sound monetary policy isn't rocket science. It's common sense, serving public interest needs, not shareholders or Wall Street profiteers seeking maximum profits for private gain.

Even if they don't know about the merits of public over privatized banking, Occupy Wall Streeters know a better way is vital. No wonder

New York protests went viral, erupting in hundreds of cities nationwide. The hacktivist "Anonymous" group urged "[e]veryone, everywhere [to occupy] their towns, their capitals and other public spaces."

This pits the collective 99% majority against "corruption, greed and inequality." The minority 1% wants privatized money power so they can get more of it. Everyone else demands change.

Putting bodies on the line despite police brutality is key. So far the sustained OWS activism has been impressive. Growing and maintaining its energy is crucial.

Famed Chicago activist Saul Alinsky (1909-1972) knew the best way to beat organized money is with organized people: "getting it altogether" for change. Calling conflict "the essential core of a free and open society," he said "[i]f one were to project the democratic way of life in the form of a musical score, its major theme would be the harmony of dissonance," working for the common good.

Its core issue is returning money power to public hands as a first step to having government of, by and for the people, serving everyone.

If that's not worth sustained struggle, what is?

A Final Comment

Wall Street-controlled money power is corrupted, corrosive and destructive. Occupy San Francisco's on the issue. On December 1, 2011, *Wall Street Journal* writer David Weidner headlined, "Occupy Shocker: A Realistic, Actionable Idea," saying:

> They have something their East Coast neighbors don't:
> a realistic plan aimed at the heart of banks. The idea
> could be expanded nationwide to send a message to a
> compromised Washington and the financial industry.

Called a municipal bank, "it would transfer the City of San Francisco's bank accounts—about $2 billion" from Bank of America, UnionBanCal and Wells Fargo—"into a public bank. [It] would use small local banks to lend to the community."

Why not! North Dakota's Bank of North Dakota has been doing it successfully since 1919. It helped the state prosper, working cooperatively with private banks. Its model can be replicated anywhere, including across America. Doing so will let all states benefit. It's an idea whose time has come!

ENDNOTES

1 Stephen Lendman, *How Wall Street Fleeces America*, Clarity Press, Inc., 2011.
2 < http://occupywallst.org/>
3 < http://www.occupytogether.org/>

2

CLASS WAR
IN AMERICA

Class war has raged in America for decades. Business and America's super-rich always win. In his 1925 short story titled "Rich Boy," F. Scott Fitzgerald said:

> Let me tell you about the very rich. They are different from you and me. They possess and enjoy early...They think, deep in their hearts, that they are better than we..
>
> Even when they enter deep into our world... they still think that that they are better than we are. They are different.

In his article, titled "The Truth About 'Class War' in America," economist Richard Wolff said: "The last 50 years have indeed seen continuous class warfare in and over federal economic policies."[1] Notably since the 1970s, "(b)usiness and its allies shifted most of its federal tax burden onto individuals."

Since WW II, tax rates on super-rich Americans fell from 91% to 35% today. Obama's deficit cutters want it lowered to 24% along with eliminating some deductions with loopholes to compensate and save others. Moreover, they want the top corporate tax rate slashed from 35% to 26%.

Many corporate giants, in fact, pay minimal or no taxes. Some, like General Electric, get generous rebates in highly profitable years. They game the system, benefitting from tax laws that they themselves write. American workers lose out by having greater than ever burdens placed on them.

Obama schemers also want deeper Medicare cuts, higher Medicaid co-pays, and Social Security's retirement age raised to 69 with lower cost-of-living increases. Privately they want Wall Street to control them to suck out maximum profits, then shut it down entirely. In addition, they want home mortgage interest and tax-free employer provided health insurance capped or ended.

Both parties represent business and the super-rich elites. America's middle class is targeted for extinction. Since taking office, Obama capitulated to Republicans on preserving tax cuts for America's super-rich. He gave trillions of dollars to Wall Street crooks and other corporate favorites, including profiteers benefitting greatly from multiple imperial wars.

At the same time, Obama stiff-armed budget-strapped states and distressed households. Promising millions of new jobs, he created none. Four years into a Main Street Depression, real unemployment approaches 23%. In ravaged cities like Detroit, it exceeds 50%. Federal workers' wages were frozen and austerity cuts were imposed, such as the Low Income Home Energy Assistance Program (LIHEAP). Families needing help to heat homes in winter won't get it. Neither will students relying on Pell Grants.

Other imposed cuts affect:

- the Children's Health Insurance Program (CHIP);

- community healthcare centers;

- nonprofit health insurance cooperatives;

- HIV/AIDS, tuberculosis, and other disease prevention programs;

- WIC (Women, Infants, and Children) grants to states for supplemental foods, healthcare, and nutrition education for low-income families;

- Head Start, providing comprehensive education, health, nutrition, and parent involvement services to low-income families with children;

- the Supplemental Nutrition Assistance Program (targeted earlier with more coming), providing food stamps for poor households;

- community development block grants for housing, overall reducing HUD's budget by $1.1 billion;

- Federal Emergency Management Agency (FEMA) first-responder funding;

- energy efficiency and renewable energy programs;

- Environmental Protection Agency (EPA) clean/safe water and other projects;

- National Institutes of Health (NIH) medical research;

- the National Park Service;

- vital infrastructure and transportation needs; and

- other non-defense discretionary spending.

These planned new cuts will help to sustain Wall Street, militarism, favoritism, waste, fraud, and other rewards for Washington's usual special interests Increasingly ordinary people are on their own to sink or swim. Obama calls it "shared sacrifice." Translated, this means: ordinary people sacrifice, business and super-rich elites share.

Washington's new FY 2012 budget agreement cuts billions more from vital domestic programs. LIHEAP lost another $1.2 billion, a 25% reduction year over year. Labor, health and education allocations dropped $1.4 billion, including $225 million cut by eliminating 22 programs, many related to job training.

In addition, Pell Grants will end for another 100,000 students, and those getting them will only receive $5,500 for another year. Overall, $1.36 billion in student funding will be lost over several years.

Corporate America's power grab holds US households hostage. Neo-serfdom and debt peonage define their agenda. Wolff calls mainstream economics "faith-based." For Michael Hudson, it's "junk economics." Nations and economies are destroyed to benefit Wall Street and powerful favorites. According to Wolff:

> In plain English, the last 50 years saw a massive shift
> of the burden of federal taxation from business to
> individuals and from rich individuals to everyone else.
> Class war policies, yes, but a war that victimized the
> vast majority of working Americans.

Especially since the 1970s, real wages haven't kept up with inflation. Benefits have steadily eroded. High-paying manufacturing and service jobs went offshore to low-wage countries. Automated production claimed more. More than ever, "free markets" work best for those who control them.

Technology-driven productivity increasingly pressures workers to toil longer for less pay and fewer benefits. Explaining predatory capitalism's contradictions, Marx rightfully called it anarchic and ungovernable. Yet what existed in his day was only a shadow of today's monster.

Predatory capitalism alienates the masses by preventing societies from developing humanely. It produces class struggles between "haves" and "have-nots," the bourgeoisie (capitalists) and proletariat (workers). It exploits the many for the elite few. Those most privileged populate Wall Street. It flourishes in America and Western societies, aided by political opportunists, powerful monopolies and oligopolies now control production, commerce and finance—and where it flourishes, ordinary people do not.Households are angered and traumatized by falling incomes lowered by inflation. As a result, more family members work harder and longer for less money. Corporate bosses extract more surplus from pressured workers.

Class war in America isn't new. Today it rages, pitting private wealth against popular interests. America's middle class is on the chopping block for destruction. The criminal class in Washington is bipartisan. Complicit with Wall Street and other corporate crooks, they've wrecked the economy and working households for profit. America's broken system is defined by sacrificing workers on the altar of capitalist excess. Growing numbers of people understand that they are trapped in a venal, depraved system too broken to fix.

It's no wonder millions now rage against it in hundreds of cities nationwide. It was just a matter of time for the American people to be galvanized. They're mad as hell and soon they won't take it anymore. They worry about no future prospects and know, or should know, that political Washington won't help.

Inequality in America has been institutionalized. Good paying jobs and retirement security are increasingly out of reach.America's kleptocracy run by corrupt politicians complicit with corporate crooks is strip-mining working households for profit. And this is just the beginning. The congressional August Budget Control Act of 2011 established the Joint Select Committee on Deficit Reduction – a.k.a. the Supercommittee. Doing so was extralegal. The Constitution's Article 1, Section 8 explains congressional powers. None of them include supercommittee authority to resolve America's debt crisis. Article 1, Section 8, Sub-section 18 lets Congress "make all Laws which shall be necessary and proper for carrying into Execution (of its other listed Powers), and all other Powers vested by this Constitution in the Government of the United States, or in any Department Officer thereof."

Even though government authority is limited only by the boundaries of possibility, no constitutional principle gives 12 members of Congress more power than others, let alone the right to exercise it secretly.Composed of six House and six Senate members from both parties, Supercommittee authority ran until November 23, 2011, holding the power to agree on $1.2 - $1.5 trillion in budget cuts over the next 10 years. Their consensus on items to be cut would have let Congress only vote them up or down without amendments, debate or delay.

Ahead of their deadline, 100 Democrats and Republicans wrote supercommittee members (the so-called "gang of 12") that "(t)o succeed, all options for mandatory and discretionary spending and revenue must be on the table." They were effectively asking for agreement on $4 trillion in cuts.

Nonetheless, hours before their self-imposed deadline, Supercommittee members ended negotiations without reaching any agreement. By law, an automatic $1.2 trillion in cuts over 10 years start in 2013.

While the cuts are supposedly to be equally divided between defense and domestic programs, you can expect sustained military spending at the expense of the gutting of America's social contract. Either way, lost purchasing power means less spending, fewer jobs, and even greater public anger than today's high levels.

It's not about political disagreements. It's about securing the interests of wealth and power. Deficit cutting always is secondary. What's key is protecting corporate handouts and Bush era tax cuts, as well as expanding them for business and upper-bracket earners.

Supercommittee Democrat members, in fact, offered unprecedented Medicare and Medicaid cuts on top of those already made—at minimum, $500 billion over the next decade with out-year increases. Social Security and public pensions are also targeted. Private ones may come later. In earlier negotiations, Obama had already agreed.

These cuts have been planned for years. Republicans want the programs eliminated. Democrats have agreed to incremental cuts to make ending core social contract programs less noticeable. This will leave seniors entirely on their own for healthcare and other benefits when they're most needed. It won't matter if they're unaffordable.

Last year, Obama's National Commission on Fiscal Responsibility and Reform (NCFRF) recommended deep Medicare cuts, higher Medicaid co-pays, and restrictions on filing malpractice suits, among other ways to end Washington's responsibility for healthcare incrementally.

The Bipartisan Policy Center (BPC) also recommended deep Medicare cuts, higher Part B premiums, big co-pays and outpatient fee increases, as well as the establishment of privately owned, lower-cost health insurance exchanges to gradually eliminate traditional Medicare. It also wants Medicaid funding cut.

Congressional Democrats and Republicans agree on raising Medicare's eligibility's age. So does Obama. He also supports deep cuts. Expect his new Independent Payment Advisory Board to recommend them. The Congressional Budget Office (CBO) said current proposals will force seniors to pay more for coverage, much more.

Medicare and Medicaid cuts are coming.. In June 2012, Vice President Biden agreed to $500 billion more in Medicare/Medicaid cuts on top of previously imposed big ones. Republicans want $780 billion cut. It's likely they will split the difference with more reductions to come later. Backloading will delay the pain until after the November 2012 elections. Both sides agree.

By mid-decade, traditional Medicare will be providing half of today's benefits. Seniors will need private plans for full coverage. Those unable to afford them will be out of luck.

Proponents falsely say Medicare, Medicaid and Social Security are responsible for rising deficits and America's national debt burden. They also bogusly claim Medicare and Social Security are going broke. When properly administered, in fact, both programs are sustainable long-term with modest adjustments and by curtailing escalating healthcare costs.

Wall Street bailouts, other corporate handouts, excess military spending (including huge black budgets), and tax cuts for the rich caused today's unsustainable debt problem. Price gouging by health insurance providers, drug companies and large hospital chains are exacerbating it

Over the past decade, Social Security-run surpluses went for debt reduction to make it appear the fund's not sustainable. In fact, since 1986, it has produced $2.4 trillion more than it spent. Much of the surplus came from increasing the payroll tax and indexing it to inflation. Its share of total federal tax revenues rose from less than 30% to 44%. At the same time, corporate income tax fell from around 20% to under 10%.

In other words, for a generation, Social Security revenues subsidized corporate handouts, tax cuts for the rich, and America's wars. Its surplus could be sustainable well into the future if government policies stopped draining it irresponsibly. Moreover, if the full payroll tax is restored and annual $108,600 income cap was lifted to make America's wealthy pay the same percentage cost as others, potential Social Security shortfalls could be eliminated for generations. If draining the trust fund also stopped, Social Security surpluses could be generated in perpetuity.

In addition, if capital gains were taxed like income, huge amounts would be raised for traditional Medicare, prescription drugs under Part D, Medicaid, and other social programs on the chopping block for big cuts or elimination.

Medicare would be just as sustainable with real healthcare reform under a universal single-payer system. By eliminating private insurer middlemen, costs would be drastically cut.

In its September 2007 report to Congress, the Congressional Research Service (CRS) compared 2004 US healthcare spending with other developed OECD (Organization for Economic Cooperation and Development) countries. It found America spent $6,102 per person (today it's over $8,000), well over double the $2,560 average for other OECD countries. Much of the difference comes from insurer administrative costs which are unrelated to providing care. In other words, other OECD countries deliver better services overall at less than half what Americans spend.

Draining Social Security's trust fund and perpetuating outlandishly high healthcare costs makes it appear that the fund which supports seniors' entitlements is going broke.

But these crisis conditions were artificially created. Congressional cassandras claim Social Security and Medicare are unsustainable because both parties want big cuts in both programs before privatizing them en route to eliminating them altogether.Political Washington hypes the problem. So do media scoundrels, Obama's Simpson/Bowles deficit cutting commission, and the Bipartisan Policy Center (BPC). Their solution is to slash, then end America's social contract in order to transfer maximum wealth to corporate favorites and the nation's super-rich.

Supercommittee negotiations stalemated over Republicans demanding big corporate and upper bracket personal income tax cuts. Both are now at 35%. Republicans want them reduced to 25-28%, so America's aristocracy will benefit from deficit reduction at the expense of working people bearing the burden.

Republicans' top priority is protecting Bush era tax cuts. Over the last decade, they cost America at least $2.9 trillion in vitally needed revenue plus another $450 billion in 2010-2012 extensions. If these tax cuts are maintained for another decade, a projected $2.2 to $2.7 trillion more will be lost, exacerbating today's debt problem.

By proposing further corporate and upper-bracket cuts, Republicans clearly aren't concerned about deficits and debt: they and most Democrats simply want corporate friends and super-rich elites protected. Congressional disagreement is only about when cuts are made, not about the amounts to be cut, or who pays for it, and who benefits. They don't just want to assure that Bush era cuts are preserved—they want to sweeten the pot.

Obama's fully on board. So are growing numbers of Democrats. They're corporatists, not populists. They talk tough, then do something else. The pattern repeats endlessly to transfer enormous wealth to corporate favorites and America's super-rich.

Medicare Privatization Plans

The idea's been around for years. More recently, bipartisan support's been growing. Various plans have circulated.

A 2006 Congressional Budget Office (CBO) study[2] assessed "Designing a Premium Support System (PSS) for Medicare." It discussed pros, cons, other choices and implications in terms of costs and recipient benefits.

In 1995, Henry Aaron and Robert Reischauer had first proposed a PSS based on managed competition principles. Numerous variations followed with differing public support amounts. All plans have six common features:

(1) Beneficiaries would choose from multiple approved health plans. Risk adjusted payments and marketing practices would be regulated, or so it's claimed.

(2) Plans would offer a premium bid to cover core benefits.

(3) Federal payments would reflect these bids, subject to negotiations.

(4) Washington would provide beneficiaries a fixed premium subsidy tied to annual health plan bids.

(5) They would vary depending on plans selected. Beneficiaries would pay differential costs.

(6) Traditional Medicare would compete on similar terms with private plans, including on price.

A March 1999, Bipartisan Commission on the Future of Medicare approved a premium support plan proposed by then-Commission chairman Senator John Breaux. Though it failed to get a supermajority needed for official recommendation to Congress, it gained widespread support and became a prominent option in subsequent Medicare reform debates.

Proponents claim it relies on marketplace medicine to secure sustainability for the longterm. They falsely say Medicare, Medicaid and Social Security cause rising deficits and America's national debt burden. They also bogusly claim Medicare and Social Security are going broke when, if properly administered, both programs are sustainable with modest adjustments and by curtailing escalating healthcare costs responsibly.

If capital gains were taxed like income, huge amounts would be raised for traditional Medicare, prescription drugs under Part D, Medicaid, and other social programs. Instead, they're on the chopping block for big cuts before privatization en route to eliminating them altogether.

In contrast, under a universal single-payer system, Medicare would be sustainable long-term. Eliminating private insurer middlemen alone achieves dramatic cost savings.

Instead of responsible workable policies, premium support and similar plans are steps toward destroying Medicare altogether, first by privatizing it for profit. Breaux's plan set federal premium subsidies at 88% of the nationally weighted average.

Beneficiaries choosing plans costing less than 85% of the average would pay no premium. Those selecting higher benefit plans would cover extra charges. Plans (allegedly) would have to provide benefits equal to current Medicare coverage, though they could offer additional benefits. They'd also be updated annually based on individual choice. Savings are alleged to come from beneficiaries selecting lower cost options, price competition to attract enrollees, and letting recipients purchase Medigap coverage for added benefits.

Reality differs markedly from these claims. Only universal coverage achieves major savings. Alternatives don't. Independent studies confirm it. Physicians for a National Health Program (PNHP)[3] says America spends double the developed world's healthcare average, yet performs poorly on key indicators like life expectancy, infant mortality, and overall well-being.

Currently, middlemen insurers, drug giants and large hospital chains game the system hugely for profits. Medicare for all can change that effectively and achieve major cost savings.

Overall, US healthcare could make a quantum improvement leap compared to today's dysfunctional system. Instead, bipartisan complicity has worse in mind by cutting benefits, placing greater burdens on seniors and others, letting corporate predators game the system, and still leave millions uninsured, on their own and out of luck.

Other Destructive Medicare Plans

On December 16, the Brookings Institution published "Premium Support: A Primer," claiming"The major cause of the federal budget crisis, which is still in its early stages, is the relentless growth of Medicare spending."[4] This, it says, is due to baby boomer retirements and "persistent increase" in per person costs:

> Unless something is one, Medicare....will grow from 3.6 percent of the nation's GDP in 2010 to 10.4 percent by 2080...
> Unchecked, growth in spending on Medicare and interest on the federal debt will bankrupt the country

Five Brookings participants were involved, including Henry Aaron, Alice Rivlin and former Republican Senator Pete Domenici. He and Rivlin also co-chair the Bipartisan Policy Center (BPC) discussed above briefly. Their "Restoring America's Future" plan will destroy it for the millions who will be greatly harmed or entirely left out by their proposals. These include:

- indexing Social Security benefits to life expectancy to reduce them as longevity increases;

- eliminating annual cost-of-living adjustments (COLAs), bogusly claiming that inflation is overstated when in fact, it far exceeds official numbers, especially in relation to medical expenses, placing enormous burdens on recipients, including retirees dependent on help;

- instituting a one-year payroll tax holiday for workers and employers to save $650 billion, which is hugely destructive since it drains revenues needed to support the entitlements;

- sharply cutting Medicare and Medicaid benefits by raising premiums, co-pays, and outpatient fees; also establishing privately owned health insurance exchanges to compete with traditional Medicare;

- cutting Medicaid by 2018 by the amount it exceeds GDP growth so needy recipients get less en route to maybe getting nothing;

- shielding insurers and drug giants from malpractice suits by making it harder to file them; then capping non-economic and punitive damage awards by adjudicating claims in "specialized malpractice courts" set up to consider the situation of providers over that of consumers;

- simplifying the tax code to two brackets (15 and 27%), which will favor the rich insofar as it will cut the top personal and corporate tax rate from 35% to 27%;

- eliminating home mortgage and most other tax deductions and credits;

- taxing employer-provided health insurance;

- instituting a 6.5% national sales tax, hitting ordinary people hardest; and

- other regressive schemes, placing added burdens on households least able to cope.

Yet BPC outrageously claims their plan "provides a comprehensive, viable path to restore our economy and build a strong America for future generations and for those around the world who look to the United States for leadership and hope."

Dominici is a former US senator. Rivlin once headed the Office of Management and Budget and the Congressional Budget Office. Is that they don't understand economics and finance enough to propose workable, constructive policies—or simply that their class bias and interest makes them put on blinders? Their proposal like others, including the one by Brookings, enriches corporate predators and America's super-rich at the expense of all others. In other words, it's another giant wealth transfer scheme, heading the nation for third world status.

So is a new bipartisan congressional one Senator Ron Wyden (D. OR) and Romney running-mate Paul Ryan (R. WI) proposed to replace traditional Medicare with "premium support" plans.

It's all about eventual privatization to free Washington from future obligations. As explained above, beneficiaries would get fixed amounts to purchase private coverage through a federally regulated Medicare exchange. Initially, traditional Medicare would remain optional. But again, in the long term it will transition to an entirely privately run system. Doing so will put vital care out of reach for millions of seniors when they most need it.

The plan closely follows Ryan's April proposal to transition Medicare toward fixed-sum vouchers. He, other Republicans, and growing numbers of Democrats want government responsibility entirely ended. His new plan temporarily lets it compete with private plans with beneficiaries incurring greater costs.

A Final Comment

No matter how much Obama and congressional Democrats tread lightly around this sensitive issue prior to the 2012 elections, post-election, traditional Medicare, Medicaid, Social Security and public pensions will be on the chopping block for elimination.

Privatizations will precede it. Eventually the military-governmental elites will be entirely able to free trillions more dollars for war-making and corporate handouts.

Safety net protections will disappear. Americans will be left on their own entirely, to sink or swim. With one-third of US households impoverished or nearly so, imagine how irresponsible governance will gravely harm millions more.

If the business of America became peace, with less militarism, no wars, making friends, not enemies, retaining high-paying/good benefit jobs at home, letting unions bargain collectively with management on equal terms, making universal free education and single-payer healthcare priorities, ending destructive trade deals, and guaranteeing living wage security, imagine how different things could be.

In addition, if money power returned to public hands and direct democracy serving everyone responsibly replaced duopoly power, near utopian conditions might be realized.

Anything is possible when committed people work long-term for them. If that's not incentive enough, what is?

America's no longer fit to live in. If there's going to be any change, we need a complete reorientation. Here are some of the vital tasks::

- making social justice a priority consideration in all new policies;

- returning money power to public hands as the Constitution's Article 1, Section 8 mandates;

- dismantling duopoly political power, replacing it with an entirely new multi-party democracy;

- getting money out of politics;

- shutting down insolvent banks andprohibiting too-big-to-fail ones;

- ending corporate personhood in the recognition that corporations are businesses, not people;

- reinstituting anti-trust laws with teeth, prohibiting monopoly and oligopoly power;

- breaking up big media;

- making broadcasting a public utility on airwaves belonging equally to everyone, not just to business giants to exploit with generous subsidies;

- prohibiting all corporate handouts, loopholes, and special benefits;

- making corporations and rich Americans pay their fair share, including a Tobin tax on large financial transactions;

- ending America's student loan racket;

- mandating progressive taxation, including treating income and capital gains equally;

- re-energizing organized labor;

- ending inequality and persecution;

- legislating living wages;

- stressing environmental sanity; and

- ending America's imperial wars.

Hopefully OWS protesters understand that dark forces want to co-opt and subvert them. Hopefully they'll focus on what matters most. What is key is to get money power in public hands and make banking a regulated public utility. Achieving that makes social justice and other vital goals possible. Millions of Americans and others globally are committed to social change. Hopefully they know they're in the mother of all struggles and will stay the course. That's how all great victories are won.

ENDNOTES

1   < http://truth-out.org/news/item/3513:the-truth-about-class-war-in-america>

2   < http://www.cbo.gov/publication/18258>

3   < http://www.pnhp.org/facts/single-payer-resources>

4   <http://www.brookings.edu/research/papers/2011/12/16-premium-support-primer>

3

THE
AUSTERITY
HOAX

Since 2008, Western nations have force-fed their people austerity poison. As a result, decline replaces prosperity, millions suffer and living standards deteriorate. Societies become no longer fit to live in.

Neoliberal and imperial priorities have let essential public needs go begging..The longer fiscal pain continues, the closer an ultimate day of reckoning approaches, likely disruptively, as people recognize that elections—throwing the bums out only to see them replaced by new ones—accomplish nothing.

America is Exhibit A for how this process works. Political Washington is corrupt, immoral, degenerate, and unprincipled. Instead of helping the American people, they destroy them. They actually benefit from imposing misery. Allied with criminal bankers and other corporate predators, politicians' policies have made conditions for growing millions intolerable.

It's well known that imperial wars destroy nations. Austerity leaves "nothing to drive the economy," as Paul Craig Roberts says. Washington's solution is to increase the wars America is fighting. Why, when it is clearly economically destructive? Because bankers, other corporate favorites, and war profiteers benefit.

Michael Hudson says austerity sacrifices the "production economy, the consumption economy, (and) the real economy...." Viable alternatives are ignored to benefit privileged elites at the expense of most others.Hudson calls it "financial warfare against the entire society, not only against labor, but against industry and, most of all, against government."Productive "industrial capitalism" has now morphed into predatory "finance capitalism." It's not financing industry. Instead, it's furthering "economic parasitism and overhead."[1]Politicians in Washington support it. Obama exceeds the worst of Bush, what will happen under Romney would be a thing of nightmares.

Europe is corrupted the same way. London's Olympiad spectacle highlighted it. At a time of high unemployment and growing public needs, estimates of $19 billion to double that amount went for the city's biggest ever extravaganza. Combined with Britain's war budget and fealty to banking crooks, it reveals a society heading for terminal decline and taking innocent people with it.The same holds for America and other European countries. Bankers rape them financially. Predatory finance is a new form of warfare, more destructive than standing armies.

Former bank regulator/financial fraud expert Bill Black addressed the issue. He headlined "The Right's Schadenfreude as their Austerity Polices Devastate Europe,"[2] saying that hisarticle followed his reading of Anne Applebaum's September 13, 2010 column, where she celebrated Britain's embrace of austerity and Tory conservatives.Applebaum headlined "Less, Please," saying that UK slash and burn "vicious cuts" are good. Austerity "made Britain great." It "won the war." It's their "finest hour."

> Then, on July 25, 2012, Applebaum's Washington Post article had headlined "Europe must face up to ongoing euro crisis". Applebaum wrote:Finally, Europeans are being forced to face up to decades' worth of fundamentally dishonest politics...
> Since the 1970s, one government after the next has spent, borrowed and then inflated its way out of the subsequent debt...
> Then they recovered—only to spend, borrow and inflate once again.[3]

She called euro straightjacket entrapment a gold standard equivalent. Losing monetary and fiscal control is good, she claims. So is abdicating national sovereignty. Applebaum economics makes witch doctor medicine look miraculous. Applebaum grew up in wealth. She attended Yale and the London School of Economics. She was admitted to Phi Beta Kappa and graduated from Yale summa cum laude. Perhaps its standards aren't as high as people think.

Let-them-eat-cake economics doesn't work. It sparks revolutions which don't turn out much better. After America's, everything changed but stayed the same. The Russians got Joseph Stalin after theirs. The French got the Jacobins, who were revolutionary moderate patriots at first. Then they morphed into "reign of terror" extremists. Dickens' *Tale of Two Cities* wrote about the best and worst of times. Liberté, egalité and fraternité were short-lived.

Sustained Applebaum economics may spark the worst of times without the best. But let us return to Bill Black, who went on to destroy her position, pointing out how austerity caused Britain›s worst economic crisis in 50 years. "Applebaum›s 2010 column on [Britain's] embrace of austerity deserves to live in infamy," he said. She "takes palpable glee [in] harming its working class" to let wealthy Brits grow richer.

In 2009, Britain was emerging from recession, with its recovery painful and slow. Ordinary people benefitted little. Many, in fact, did not benefit at all. The modest stimulus injected then was grossly inadequate, ensuring further economic decline.

Austerity represents bad economics and moral failure. Reality is turned on its head. Nations aren't "remotely like households when it comes to debt," Black went on. They "adopt ‹automatic stabilizers› to make recessions far less severe and recoveries quicker." They work. They›re counter-cyclical. Austerity makes bad conditions worse.

Applebaum equates austerity with "moral superiority." The greater the amount, the higher the level of morality. This explains her reveling in "savage cuts" and "delightin gore." Effectively, it's a belief that moral superiority depends on how much harm can be imposed on society's most disadvantaged. Notions this destructive reflect Frankenstein economics. Pain is good, the more the better. Wealthy elites love it. British politics is like America›s where the Democrats don›t differ from Republicans. In the UK, Tories and New Labour replicate each other›s policies. Let-'em-eat cake is dogma.

As a result, Britannia›s ship of state is sinking. So is the American dream. For most, it was largely an illusion. Now it's disappearing entirely. Again to Black: "Applebaum also combines faux moral superiority with faux history." She uses it "to explain the moral virtues of austerity during a Great Recession."

Claiming austerity won the war is rubbish. Massive fiscal stimulus and deficits won the war. UK and US politicians claim their governments are broke. If foreign aggressors invaded their homelands, asked Black, would they surrender for lack of funds?" Of course not, they would run however large a deficit was required. Because that doesn't destroy economies, it stimulates growth and produces full employment.

War economies ended the Great Depression. Comparable stimulus *without war* could reverse similar conditions that affect majorities in Europe and America today. Productive policies lift all boats.

Nations enduring hard times "cannot simply 'decide' to end [their] budget deficit." Combining spending cuts with higher taxes on working households assures harder times.

Legitimate economists don't recommend spending cuts and higher taxes. Sustained policies this destructive assure protracted or permanent decline. Britain, other EU countries, and America can borrow at near-zero interest rates. Every pound, euro and dollar raised and spent productively returns multiples more. It's immoral not to do it when it's most needed, when privileged elites alone benefit at the expense of most others.

For the governments to claim empty pockets is duplicitous. Applebaum's prime targets are Medicare, Medicaid and Social Security. Destroying bedrock social safety net protections is scandalous. But then, she's privileged and doesn't care. Other elitists feel the same way. Programs people can't do without are on their chopping block for elimination. The more ordinary people suffer, the greater elitists benefit.

Promoting social inequality is the very definition of immorality. It's also destructive economics. Applebaum "reveal(ed) her real target— she wants to destroy (bedrock) social programs." She considers them "political bribes to induce the working class to vote for leftist politicians." But social programs improve millions of lives. They also lift all boats. The resultant prosperity produces jobs. When people have money they spend it. Hard times forces belt-tightening, forces working people to accept conditions and wages that otherwise they would resist.

Accordingly, Appelbaum loves the euro straightjacket rules and Troika diktat authority over independent monetary and fiscal control as well as national sovereignty. She "loves the euro zone disaster her austerity policies generated because she believes (it) will destroy the social programs she despises," and "bring the extreme right to power."

It's an agenda the Trilateralists and Bilderberger elites promote to further their aim of global rule with their version of aclassless society: one with only rulers and serfs. She's wrong, says Black. Things won't turn out her way.

Obama embraces the worst of what Applebaum and Republicans endorse. Black thinks he'll "pay a great political price for trying to be all things to all voters on the issue of austerity" alone.Opposing it should have been his "signature economic program." Winning by a landslide would be assured. Instead, administration policies are "incoherent" and counterproductive.

Why didn't he do it?

ENDNOTES

1   <http://www.nakedcapitalism.com/2012/04/michael-hudson-on-why-there-is-an-alternative-to-european-austerity.html>

2   < http://www.nakedcapitalism.com/2012/07/bill-black-the-rights-schadenfreude-as-their-austerity-policies-devastate-europe.
html?utm_source=feedburner&utm_medium=email&utm_campa
ign=Feed%3A+NakedCapitalism+%28naked+capitalism%29&u
tm_content=Yahoo%21+Mail>

3   < http://www.washingtonpost.com/opinions/anne-applebaum-europe-must-face-up-to-ongoing-euro-crisis/2012/07/25/gJQAnYey9W_story.
html>

4

TRILLIONS STASHED
IN TAX HAVENS

A new Tax Justice Network (TJN) USA report reveals an estimated $21-$32 trillion of hidden and stolen wealth stashed largely tax-free secretly. Titled "The Price of Offshore Revisited,"[1] it explains what financial insiders know but won't discuss. Many of them have their own hidden wealth. TJN describes a "subterranean" systemic "economic equivalent of an astrophysical black hole." The higher estimate above exceeds US GDP twofold.

It's mind-boggling. It's hard to imagine that a tiny percent of privileged elites control this much wealth secretly. It's worse knowing it's largely tax free. It's appalling that governments let them get away with it.

Wall Street and other major banks manage that wealth. Their business is fraud and grand theft. Private banking operations yield huge profits. Their ability to keep funds secreted tax free attracts rich clients. Private capital globally is attracted. It's welcome from anyone, from everywhere, "no questions asked."

Government policies protect them. Societal costs are huge. Tax justice is absent. Hotel magnate Leona Helmsley once said only little people pay taxes. TJN's report bears her out. The Report addresses avast "global offshore industry", largely tax-free, controlled by the world's richest, most powerful elites.

Estimating the amounts they have secreted takes tedious data mining. Previous estimates relied more on rough judgments But TJN has surpassed this. TJN used several methods. They include available data sources, estimation methods, and core assumptions. They're open to peer review and public scrutiny. Only financial wealth is included. Much else isn't measured. It includes real estate, yachts, racehorses, gold, art, and other categories not easily quantified

Here are the four key approaches TJN used:

(1) A "sources-and-uses" country-by-country model.

(2) An "accumulated offshore wealth" model.

(3) An "offshore investor portfolio" model.

(4) Best-guess estimates of offshore assets held by the world's top 50 private banks.

Familiar Wall Street, European, and other global financial institutions are the targets of investigation. Current data from global central banks, the World Bank, IMF, UN, and national accounts were used. Other evidence includes:

(1) "Transfer mispricing" data.

(2) Demand for cross-border liquid "mattress money" data.

(3) Current research data on the offshore private banking market's size.

TJN believes its work comprises the "most rigorous and comprehensive" data ever produced. It challenges anyone to contest it..In overall size through 2010, TJN estimates hidden global wealth at from $21 to $32 trillion, invested "virtually tax-free" through a still-expanding black hole of more than 80 secret jurisdictions. TJN calls its estimates conservative.Developed countries have huge offshore tax evasion problems. Repatriation would reduce their debt substantially. In fact, doing so would bring it well within tolerable levels. The offshore economy alone has an enormous negative impact on the domestic tax bases of affected countries. They've had significant private capital outflows for decades or longer.

TJN focused on 139 countries, mainly "low-middle income" ones on whom the World Bank and IMF maintain data. Since the 1970s, private bankers let rich elites in these countries accumulate trillions in hidden wealth even as their nations experienced harsh structural adjustments. They became debt-entrapped. Some borrowed themselves into insolvency, selling off public assets at fire sale prices and impoverishing their peoples. They colluded with big money interests at their expense.

Through 2010, these countries accumulated over $4 trillion in debt—minus foreign reserves invested in First World securities, it's $2.8 trillion. Including hidden wealth, they're net lenders.

The key factor is that the assets of these countries are held by wealthy elites while ordinary people bear the burden of debts. In the 1980s, an unnamed Fed official said: "The problem is not that these countries don't have any assets. The problem is they're all in Miami"[2] and other global cities. They're home to private financial institutions.

Hidden offshore wealth correlates positively with loan amounts to indebted countries. Large amounts of borrowed capital were secreted lawlessly in global tax havens. Local elites continue "vot(ing) with financial feet" at the same time as their public sectors borrow heavily and ordinary people go begging.

Although First World countries borrow most, they and the elites in them remain global financiers. Overall, wealth is concentrated in select private hands "in a handful of source countries," many of which are regarded as debtors.

Through 2010, 50 top private banks managed over $12 trillion in cross-border assets from individual clients, trusts and foundations. Smaller banks, investment firms, insurers, and non-bank intermediaries like hedge funds and independent money managers handle additional amounts up to an overall $32 trillion estimate. TJN calls these enablers part of a global "tax injustice system." Complicit governments let them operate at the expense of their own people. They write:"Since the late 1970s, investigative journalists, tax authorities, drug enforcement officials, terrorist trackers, national security experts," and others became aware about vast amounts of money stashed in "offshore" tax havens.

Private banking "professional enablers" manage these funds, making make fortunes doing so. The term "offshore" refers less to physical locations than to virtual ones anywhere—often "networks of legal and quasi-legal entities and arrangements" operating in the interests of money managers. Their physical locations can be anywhere. Legal structures typically are assets owned by anonymous offshore companies in one jurisdiction. Trusts are in another. Trustees are in multiple places globally.

Their clients are rich elites, corporations, and criminals. They include real estate speculators, technology tycoons, oil sheiks, underworld millionaires, heads of state, despots, and drug lords, among others. Their common needs include:

(1) Anonymity and confidentiality.

(2) Minimizing or avoiding taxes.

(3) Skilled money management.

(4) Ability to access and manage their wealth from anywhere.

(5) Secure places to reside, visit, or hide.

(6) Assured financial security no matter what's happening in the real world.

Skilled professionals provide these services globally. Money management happens in a virtual world. They live under one set of rules. Another exists for all others Physical locations are based in Bermuda, the Cayman Islands, Nauru, St. Kitts, Antigua, Tortola, Switzerland, the Channel Islands, Monaco, Cyprus, Gibraltar, Liechtenstein, and elsewhere Over 3.5 million paper companies, thousands of shell banks and insurers, more than half the world's registered commercial ships above 100 tons, and tens of thousands of shell subsidiaries of giant global banks, accounting firms, and various other companies are registered as operating from there.

Nonetheless, conventional havens are misleading. Despite their vast financial infrastructure, most super-rich elites want more security. They also need easy access to First World capital markets, competent attorneys and accountants, independent judiciaries, and laws protecting them. The professional "enablers" provide all these needed services. Managing vast wealth is complex. Many skills are required. They include financial, economic, legal, accounting, and insurance. Super-rich elites demand and get the best.

Haven locations offer more than tax avoidance. Almost anything goes, including fraud, bribery, illegal gambling, money laundering, human and sex trafficking, arms dealing, toxic waste dumping, conflict diamonds and endangered species trafficking, bootlegged software, and endless other lawless practices.

It's impossible to estimate the total lawful and illegal wealth from all sources. It's vastly more than estimates within the parameters of TJN's study. Credit Suisse tried. Through mid-2011, Credit Suisse put total financial and non-financial global wealth at $231 trillion. This best guess is tenfold TJN's top figure, roughly 3.5 times global GDP. In 2011, it was about $65 trillion.

Imagine the good a small percentage of global wealth could do for billions of disadvantaged people. Imagine its ability to stabilize and recapitalize troubled countries. Imagine a world where everyone shares its wealth. Imagine one worth living in.

Global wealth represents low-hanging fruit that is nonetheless— at this time—out of reach. It's an injustice that begs for transformational change. From the bottom up is the only way possible.

Shedding light on what's dark is a good way to start.

5

LIBOR SCANDAL REFLECTS A CESSPOOL OF FINANCIAL FRAUD

At issue is a bad barrel, not a few rotten apples. Western banking is rife with fraud. The business model of major banks is grand theft. The scandal surrounding the London Inter-Bank Offer Rate (LIBOR), the interest rate that banks charge each other for loans, is just the latest.

According to Paul Craig Roberts,[1] Libor rigging is permitted in order to prop up a system that might fail without it. Imagine! The global financial system actually *needs fraud* to keep on operating. It hardly matters what harm it causes.

Libor is only one part of "the interest rate rigging scandal," explained Roberts. The Fed rigs rates. How else could debt issuances yield negative returns in terms of inflation? Unrestrained financial chicanery caused today's crisis. Self-regulating markets commit fraud with impunity. The incentives to do it are embedded in it.

Resolving today's crisis involves restoring regulatory sanity. A corporate/government conspiracy prevents it. Problems fester and worsen. How long can "negative interest rates continue while debt explodes upward?" Avoiding "armageddon" should be prioritized.

Like terrorist threats used to destroy freedoms, financial crisis conditions have the Fed, ECB, Bank of England, and Bank of Japan operating "far outside [their] charter[s] and normal ... behavior." What's ongoing is "irresponsible and thoughtless," says Roberts. Years of financialization, deregulation, and manipulation "caused a financial crisis" only fraud can manage.

Imagine economies sustained by grand theft. Imagine harming most people in it so a privileged few can prosper. Imagine an unholy government/business alliance that makes it necessary and legal. Imagine media scoundrels ignoring it. Imagine an eventual day of reckoning. All

Ponzi schemes collapse. Some go on interminably before imploding. This one long ago outlived its normal lifespan. It's on borrowed time. When it goes, watch out.

Thankfully, public banking solutions await. Over a century ago, William Jennings Brown explained fraudsters

> tell us that the issue of paper money is a function of the bank and that the government ought to go out of the banking business ... I stand with Jefferson [and say] as he did, that the issue of money is a function of the government and that the banks should go out of the governing business.
>
> [W]hen we have restored the money of the Constitution, all other necessary reforms will be possible, and....until that is done there is no reform that can be accomplished.

Contrast what he endorsed with what goes on today. Bankers systematically plunder economies for their own self-enrichment. Complicit politicians let them.

UK-based Barclays bank was caught in a Libor rigging scandal. Other major banks are involved. Expect more to come out. How much and who's named remains to be seen. More on that below.

Libor and Euribor are mechanisms used to set interest rates. Libor is the fundamental short-term rate-setting benchmark. It's set daily between UK banks for overnight to 12 month durations. Produced for ten currencies with 15 maturities, it represents the London market's lowest cost of unsecured funding.

Since the 1980s, the Libor expanded exponentially in importance. London's status grew as an international financial center to become the world's largest. Over 20% of all international bank lending occurs there and more than 30% of all foreign exchange transactions. Over 240 of the world's largest banks operate key parts of their international business in London. It's the world's "cowboy finance capital," says economist Jack Rasmus.

In the 1980s, as demand grew for an accurate measure of the real rate at which banks and other financial institutions could borrow from each other, the Libor grew in importance It affects the price and availability of capital. The higher the Libor goes, the greater the borrowing cost for businesses, individuals, real estate and other loans.

The Libor anchors multi-trillion-dollar contracts. One analyst said it's like plumbing: when it's working well, it isn't noticed. When not, all hell breaks loose. It's a vital factor in the interest rate swaps market. These devices let one bank or other organization pay a fixed rate of interest on a given amount of money from another financial institution While in return, that other bank or organization pays a floating rate based on the Libor.

The global swaps market approaches $350 trillion. According to the Bank for International Settlements:

- [I]nterest rate swaps are the largest component of the global OTC derivatives market.

- The notional amount outstanding as of June 2009 in OTC interest rate swaps was $342 trillion, up from $310 trillion in Dec 2007.

- The gross market value was $13.9 trillion in June 2009, up from $6.2 trillion in Dec 2007.

In theory, credit default swaps let lenders and borrowers minimize the risk of interest rate changes. It doesn't always work that way. Nonetheless, without a mechanism in place, banks might not lend at fixed rates. Their payments to depositors are based on floating rates. If rates rise, so do costs. If they exceed revenues, crises follow.

Predatory Capitalism Failed

Rodney Shakespeare is Professor of Binary Economics at Trisakti University, Britain. He's a financial expert and a regular on the Progressive Radio News Hour. Shakespeares aid Libor rigging affects "a thousand trillion dollars" in contracts of one sort or other globally. It exceeds global GDP 15 or 20-fold.

Barclays may be at the center of the storm in the UK, but it reflects a corrupt system, with much still to be exposed. Other major banks operate the same way. They're failing. They're zombie banks. The entire system is corrupt and crumbling. Western politicians permit it. As Shakespeare says, "They uphold the doctrine that whatever banks do is right."

The seriousness of what's known is that a system portrayed as just and sound in actuality is failing due to rampant speculation at the expense of stimulating real economic growth.Casino capitalism doesn't work. Economies suffer from their operations, and so do ordinary people. The entire banking system risks collapse.. Barclays is part of a far greater unresolved problem. All that can be done is to buy time. The system is too corrupt to fix.

John McMurtry calls the financial system a cancer system. The longer it goes unaddressed, the worst things get. "Organic, social and ecological life" harm grows. Effectively, it's aife-system collapse. Societies are consumed by it. Humanity suffers. It needs to be cleared out and replaced with an entirely new paradigm. Central bankers and complicit politicians bear full responsibility for what's happening. They're heading economies for a worse disaster than the Great Depression.

Last February, the Wall Street Journal headlined "Traders Manipulated Key Rate, Bank says,"[2] saying that according to an Ottawa court filing,

> Canada's Competition Bureau said a bank it didn't identify has told the agency's investigators that people involved in the alleged scheme 'were able to move' interest rates...
>
> People familiar with the [scheme] said the 'cooperating party' is [Switzerland-based] UBS AG.

An investigation into the Libor rigging issue affected banks and traders in North America, Europe and Asia. No one was charged with wrongdoing. Documents said regulators were also examining "alleged attempts to fix the prices of certain derivative financial products linked to Libor." Parties involved "entered into agreements to submit artificially high or artificially low" quotes. Traders "used emails and instant messages to tell each other whether they wanted 'to see a higher or lower yen Libor [rate] to aid their trading position,' according to court documents." Traders "would then 'communicate internally' with the person at their bank who was responsible for submitting the Libor quote, before letting each other know if this attempt to influence the quote had worked."

The Canadian watchdog said six banks were involved: Citigroup, Deutsche Bank, HSBC, JP Morgan Chase, Royal Bank of Scotland, and UBS.

All major banks commit grand theft. It's standard practice. Corrupt politicians turn a blind eye. So do regulators. Western banking is rife with fraud. All markets are manipulated up or down for profit. Enormous amounts are made. Governments and banks collude. High volume program trading drives prices either way. Nothing gets reported unless scandals erupt. In the meantime, ordinary investors who are none the wiser get trampled.

Financial history includes many examples of major financial institutions getting a free lunch at the public's expense. Methods include market manipulation, insider trading, front-running, theft and conspiracy, misrepresentation, Ponzi schemes, false accounting, embezzling, appointing industry favorites as regulators, tax frauds, profiting from loans that fail, creating phony financial products, and overall, assuring world financial capitals are banker occupied territories.

Barclays is the tip of the current scandal. Traders in London, New York and Tokyo also colluded to manipulate Libor. Top executives and traders are involved. They bear full responsibility for the 2008 financial crisis and what followed. They're up to their ears in fraud today. Media scoundrels cover it all up by projecting an illusion of stability. Government probes are toothless.

A City of Baltimore/Charles Schwab et al class action lawsuit names Barclays, RBS, HSBC, Bank of America, Citigroup, JPMorgan Chase, UBS and Deutsche Bank. Perhaps future suits will charge Goldman Sachs, Wells Fargo, and major European banks not named above, since they're all in it together. CEOs and other top executives conspire with each other and traders to commit fraud. Why not, when corrupt politicians wink and nod and let them do it.

Bill Black says manipulating Libor is easy. What's coming out reflects "the largest rigging of prices in the history of the world by many orders of magnitude." Top executives are directly involved: they have to be, because they set the policy and stand to gain hugely from the fraud-driven profits.

To give you an idea of the volumes involved, the US Commodity Futures Trading Commission (CTFC) says:

> US dollar Libor is the basis for the settlement of the three-month Eurodollar futures contracts traded on the Chicago Mercantile Exchange, which had a traded volume in 2011 with a notional value exceeding $564 trillion.

The *Wall Street Journal* estimates the volume at $800 trillion. These types of numbers are unfathomable. The *Financial Times* headlined "Barclays boss discussed Libor with BoE," saying:

> The bank admitted that it lowballed estimates of its borrowing costs from late 2007 to May 2009 because it wanted to reassure investors of its strength during the financial crisis and it believed other banks were doing the same.
> It also admitted that its traders improperly influenced the rate submissions from 2005 to 2008 to make money on derivatives.[3]

On the one hand, said Barclays, rogue traders committed fraud. On the other, bank executives submitted lower daily Libor rates than true costs to assure higher profits.

In the wake of the scandal, Chairman Marcus Agius and CEO Bob Diamond resigned. They and other banking crooks should be prosecuted and imprisoned. Since banker-caused crisis conditions erupted in fall 2007, no senior executive has faced charges. Expect none now to be held criminally liable. At most complicit banks are assessed hand-slap fines. They're then free to steal again. It's standard practice.

On June 30, London *Guardian* writer Will Hutton headlined "Let's end this rotten culture that only rewards rogues," saying:

> The Barclays rate-rigging scandal has once again exposed a world where men and women with little skill and no moral compass can become very rich very fast.[4]
>
> Investment banking is an organised scam masquerading as a business. It is defined by endemic conflicts of interest, systemic amoral behaviour and extreme avarice.
>
> Many of its senior figures should be serving prison sentences or disgraced—and would have been if British regulators had been weaned off the doctrine of 'light touch' regulation earlier and if the Serious Fraud Office's budget had not been emasculated by Mr. Osborne [UK Chancellor of the Exchequer].
>
> It is a tax on wealth generation and an enemy of honest endeavour—the beast that is devouring British capitalism.

It's far more than a British problem, of course. It's global, unchecked, and hugely destructive. Regulatory oversight is absent. Mary Schapiro, who heads America's SEC, turns a blind eye to fraud and abuse. She protects Wall Street, not investors. She lets banks self-regulate, and why not? She's a consummate insider. As former head of the Financial Industry Regulatory Authority (FINRA), she promoted self regulation. She also ran the National Association of Securities Dealers' (NASD) and Commodity Futures Trading Commission. She's an expert at quashing fraud investigations.

So are UK Financial Services Authority (FSA) officials. Instead of regulating, they collude. Political leaders from major parties are involved. Duopoly power runs Britain and America. Tories, New Labor, Republicans and Democrats prioritize what serves bankers. The economies of both countries are financialized. Whitehall and Washington operate the same way. They facilitate fraud. It's institutionalized. Politicians profit hugely from generous campaign contributions and high-paying jobs when leave government. Central bankers know what's going on and fuel it with bailouts and easy money.

On July 1, the London *Telegraph* headlined "Libor scandal: How I manipulated the bank borrowing rate," saying: "An anonymous insider from one of Britain's biggest lenders—aside from Barclays—explains how he and his colleagues helped manipulate the UK's bank borrowing rate. Neither the insider nor the bank can be identified for legal reasons." He gave presentations. He explained how Libor was rigged. It's easy, he said. No checks exist. Penalties for getting caught hardly matter. "[E]veryone" knows what's going on and "everyone" does it. Fraud is part of the system.

A Final Comment

Ellen Brown describes a "Wall Street Protection Racket of Covert Derivatives....Prop(ing) Up US Debt," saying: "Interest rate swaps are now over 80 percent of the massive derivatives market." Wall Street giants operate a "protection racket of a covert derivatives trade in interest rate swaps."

> The derivatives casino itself is just a last-ditch attempt to prop up a private pyramid scheme in fractional-reserve money creation, one that has progressed over several centuries through a series of "reserves"—from gold, to Fed-created "base money," to mortgage-backed securities, to sovereign debt ostensibly protected with derivatives.

The Libor is a vital factor in the swaps market. The cost of money affects them all. Privately created money at whatever interest rate bankers set "is the granddaddy of all pyramid schemes."

Despite "a quadrillion dollar derivatives edifice propping it up," eventually it will collapse. Money power in public hands could prevent it. This is an option "ready to replace the old system when it comes crashing down," says Brown.

Corrupt politicians won't return money control to public hands where it belongs ahead of time to avoid the crash. They benefit handsomely by standing pat. Why mess up a good thing by doing the right thing.

ENDNOTES

1   <http://www.globalresearch.ca/the-libor-scandal-in-full-perspective/31999>

2   "Traders Manipulated Key Rate, Bank Says", *Wall Street Journal*, February 12, 2012.

3   < http://www.ft.com/intl/cms/s/0/94a88010-c37c-11e1-966e-00144feabdc0.html>

4   < http://www.guardian.co.uk/commentisfree/2012/jun/30/will-hutton-barclays-banking-reform>

6

IMF FINANCIAL TERRORISM

In July 1944, the IMF and Bank for Reconstruction and Development (now the World Bank) were established to integrate developing nations into the global North-dominated world economy. Under the new post-war monetary system, the IMF was created to stabilize exchange rates linked to the dollar and bridge temporary payment imbalances between nations. The World Bank was to provide credit to war-torn developing countries. Both bodies, in fact, proved hugely exploitive. Instead of solving problems, they used debt entrapment to transfer public wealth to Western bankers and other corporate predators.

On a grander scale today, the scheme destructively obligates indebted nations to take new loans in order to be able to service old ones. As a result, rising indebtedness and the ability to impose structural adjustment are assured. This leads to::

- privatization of state enterprises, many sold for a fraction of their real worth;

- mass layoffs;

- deregulation;

- deep social spending cuts;

- wage freezes or cuts;

- unrestricted free market access for western corporations;

- corporate-friendly tax cuts;

- tax increases for working households;

- trade unionism suppression or marginalization; and

- harsh repression against proponents of social democracy, civil and human rights.

This enables bankers and other corporate predators to strip mine countries of their material wealth and resources. They shift them from public to private hands, crush democratic values, hollow out nations into backwaters, destroy middle class societies, and turn workers into serfs for those having means to employ them. In other words, freedom is replaced by perpetual debt bondage. The whole of humanity is consumed in a race to the bottom follows. An elite few benefit at the expense of the many. Nations are henceforth entrapped, forced to pay homage to money master kleptocrats, effectively handing over their sovereignty to foreign forces which now impose their state policies.

Neoliberalism is neo-Malthusianism writ large, destroying most of humanity to save its continuance by a few. Its holy trinity mandates: 1) no public sphere, 2) unrestrained corporate empowerment, and 3) the elimination of social spending to devote all state resources for bottom line profits, national security and internal control. Except for the privileged few, it's the worst, not the best, of all possible worlds. Economies are financialized into debt bondage, transforming them into hollow shell dystopian backwaters.

In the 1980s, 187 IMF loans caused poverty, hunger, malnutrition, disease and death for many developing countries, including all sub-Saharan ones entrapped by the structural adjustment (in the interest of western corporations) that they imposed. Their growth declined on average by 2.2% per year, and per capita income dropped below pre-independence levels. Debt service (the assurance of which is a primary aim of structural adjustment) required that health expenditures be cut by 50% and education by 25%. Moreover, as indebtedness rises, so does forced austerity, again to ensure debt service, until it becomes a self-perpetuating death spiral requiring new loans to service old ones. It's a never-ending cycle to oblivion for many nations in hock to IMF mandates.

In Latin America, the 1980s was a lost decade. Loans to Chile required 40% wage cuts. During Mexico's 1982 debt crisis, wages as well as spending for health, education, and basic infrastructure dropped by half. As a result, infant mortality tripled and vital human needs went unmet to assure that bankers got paid.

By decade's end, developing nations overallwere worse off, not better. They were deeper than ever in debt just as IMF officials had planned. Currency devaluations followed. External debts burgeoned. Growth fell. In the prior period from 1976 to 1982, Latin American borrowing had doubled. About 70% of the new loans were needed to service old ones.

Yet Article I of the IMF's Articles of Agreement audaciously if not mendaciously says it lends:

> to give confidence to members by making the general resources of the Fund temporarily available to them under adequate safeguards, thus providing them with opportunity to correct maladjustments in their balance of payments without resorting to measures destructive of national or international prosperity.The IMF's web site states it provides loans to reduce poverty and increase economic development. It adds that "[i]n difficult economic times, [it] helps countries to protect the most vulnerable in a crisis."

In fact, it does precisely the opposite. It maliciously entraps countries in debt, poverty and deprivation. It operates as the loan shark of last resort. It demands not a pound of flesh but all of it, no matter the pain and suffering caused. Once shock therapy entrapped Chile under Pinochet, unemployment rose from 9.1 to 18.7% between 1974 and 1975. At the same time, output fell 12.9% as cheap imports flooded the country. As a result, local businesses closed, hunger grew, and so did mass disenchantment with economic austerity followed by repressive crackdowns against challenges to regime control. A decade later, GDP growth resumed, but only after conditions for most of the population worsened. About 45% of Chileans were impoverished while the nation's richest 10% saw their incomes rise by 83%.

It works the same way everywhere under IMF mandates. They cause mass impoverishment, public wealth transfer to private hands, out-of-control corruption and cronyism, leaving nations transformed into backwaters to benefit the domestic and foreign super-richelites. In 1980s in Bolivia under Victor Paz Estenssoro, austerity included wage freezes, ending food subsidies, lifting price controls, hiking oil prices by 300%, imposing deep social spending cuts, permitting unrestricted imports, downsizing state enterprises before privatizing them, and letting unemployment rise sharply.

The decade through the early 1990s saw Latin American debt rise from $110 billion in 1980 to $473 in 1992. It was accompanied by interest payments growing from $6.4 billion to $18.3 billion. As a result, worker livelihoods, health and welfare suffered.

Globally, in fact, many millions lucky enough to have work endure sub-poverty wages to let foreign predators profit enormously on human misery. It's the IMF's dirty game. It spreads pain, not prosperity by lifting all boats as it proclaims. This scenario was replicated from sub-Saharan Africa to Latin America to Russia and Asian Tiger countries in 1997/98. They were looted one at a time or in combination. The IMF invasion turned Asia's economic miracle into disaster.

The International Labor Organization estimated 24 million jobs were lost as a result of selling state enterprises at fire sale prices. Western brands replaced local ones, western ownership replaced local ownership, and foreign predators benefitted from what *The New York Times* called "the world's biggest going-out-of-business sale." At the same time, Asian workers became human wreckage. IMF policy statements never explain what actually happens. Instead, they perpetuate the myth about offering help as a lender of last resort when, in fact, their mandate is to plunder for profit, no matter the damage caused.

Expect more of the same under its new managing director, Christine Lagarde. She was Washington's top choice. Treasury Secretary Tim Geithner endorsed her over Mexico's central bank governor Agustin Carstens, her only competitor after IMF's board of directors excluded Israeli central bank governor Stanley Fischer, allegedly because of age. In fact, he lacked support outside Israel, and US officials stuck with traditional IMF policy of putting a European in charge.

An American always heads the World Bank, yet Washington dominates all international lending agencies. It picks officials heading them, public rhetoric notwithstanding. On June 28, 2011 a brief IMF statement announced Lagarde's appointment, saying"The executive board of the International Monetary Fund today selected Christine Lagarde to serve as IMF managing director and madame chairman of the executive board for a five-year term starting July 2011." China, Russia and Brazil also supported her besides America and most European nations. Britain's Chancellor of the Exchequer George Osborne called it "good news for the global economy and for Britain." Then French President, Nicolas Sarkozy, said about his departing finance minister's appointment: it's a "victory for France." French banks are heavily exposed to the Greek (and other troubled nations') debt Lagarde is mandated to protect. However, more on that, below.

Lagarde's first move was to back Western banks' tough austerity demands. As she said:"If there is one message I have to send tonight, it is to say the Greek opposition must join a national entente with the party that is in power." The primary objective of IMF loans is debt service; it tops other obligations. The IMF cannot help but know—as is empirically demonstrated time after time—that austerity doesn't work to rekindle weak economies; but then, that was never the intent. Rather, austerity policies assure that bankers get paid, no matter the hardships imposed on working households through no fault of their own. It doesn't matter that bailing out European banks violates IMF charter provisions.

In his June 29, 2011 article headlined, "A World Overwhelmed by Western Hypocrisy,"[1] economist and former Reagan administration Assistant Treasury Secretary Paul Craig Roberts said the IMF "is only empowered to make balance of payments loans, but is lending to the Greek government for prohibited budgetary reasons [so it] can pay the banks." The European Central Bank (ECB) is also "prohibited from bailing out member countr[ies]," but it's doing it for the same reason. In other words, banker bottom line priorities supersede institutional rules and legal standards. It makes a mockery of both the rule of law and of governments of, by and for people—about whom they don't give a damn and show it.

On June 29, 2011, the *Wall Street Journal* said Lagarde has unsettled legal questions at home, explaining that:

> [A] French criminal court [will] decide on July 8 whether to launch a probe into accusations that [she] overstepped her authority as finance minister in 2007 when dealing with a controversy pitting tycoon Bernard Tapie against the French state, or to dismiss the case."

The case remains unresolved and may drag on for years, according to legal experts. Given broad consensus backing her, expect eventual resolution in her favor or at least nothing worse than wrist slap fines or reprimands. At issue was her 403 million euro arbitration order benefitting Tapie over France. As a result, French Court of Cassation (its highest court of appeal) Attorney General Jean-Louis Nadal ordered the Tapie dossier made public. Included in it are allegations that "Lagarde had indeed acted in a way to defeat the law... to help Tapie gain a favourable decision, against an earlier" appeals court judgment favoring the state.

Perhaps Lagarde replacing former IMF head Dominique Strauss-Kahn is old news, but it's still germane to any understanding about the organization. He was forced out over now discredited attempted rape allegations. Even at the time, it was an implausible accusation. What is more plausible is that he was targeted for backing more responsible IMF policies that were an anathema to bankers. He endorsed employment and equity as building blocks of economic stability and prosperity, political stability and peace, counter to IMF core principles, if not its public face. . As a result, he had to go.

Wall Street and other financial giants focus solely on extracting maximum wealth at the expense of working households and nations. Lagarde's expected to assure it. Expertise aside, her background shows ready willingness to comply. In 2009, the *Financial Times* called her the best Eurozone finance manager even though her background is law, not economics. The same year, *Forbes* ranked her the world's 17th most powerful woman; by 2012 she had risen to number 8.[2]

Lagarde's official/unpublicized credentials are broad and extensive. She spent her early years in America, initially in the 1970s, as an intern of Rep. William Cohen. She later served Cohen as he became Senator and then Defense Secretary under Clinton. In 1981, she joined Baker & McKenzie (B & K) in Chicago—a major international law firm practicing antitrust and labor law—and made a career in the United States.[3] In 1995, she was elevated to its Executive Committee then in October 1999, she was appointed chairman of B & K's Global Executive Committee. From 1995-1998, she chaired B & K's European Regional Council and Professional Development Committee. In 2004 and 2005, she was an ING Groep NV Supervisory Group member, and in 2004, she became president of its Strategy Committee. She spent over two decades at B & K before returning to France as de Villepin's trade minister. She also served as Board of Governors chairman for the European Bank for Reconstruction and Development, as well as a Board of Governors member at the European Investment Bank and Inter-American Development Bank.

Other information excluded from her official resume includes her membership in America's Center for Strategic & International Studies (CSIS)—an influential organization emphasizing national security and "advancing [US] global interests." Specializing in crisis management, it's also connected to the highest government and Pentagon levels. There and later, Lagarde put their interests above those of France, including while heading (with Zbigniew Brzezinski from 1995-2002) the USA-Poland Defense Industries working group.At B & K, she noticeably favored US corporate interests over French ones, including Boeing and Lockheed-Martin at the expense of Airbus and Dassault. In 2003, she became a member of the Commission for the Expansion of the Euro-Atlantic Community, in charge of potential Poland, Latvia, Romania, Czech Republic and Hungary investments.

For many years, Lagarde was a walking conflict of interests. When the political positions of groups she represented are considered, it's impossible to ignore how completely opposite they are from the French positions defended by her former boss, de Villepin. Lagarde promoted US business interests, not those of France. In his May 30, 2011 *CounterPunch* article, titled "The IMF After Strauss-Kahn," Philippe Marliere, a University of London Professor of French and European politics, noted that while she may have served as Sarkozy's finance minister, it was "hard to find one single decision, debate or policy that she has initiated or imposed her mark on. At home, her voice has hardly been heard in economic debates, let alone in political debates in general."

No matter, she's a player, a club member in good standing, a neoliberal hardliner. As a result, she was chosen to enforce structural adjustment austerity, starting with Greece.

On July 5, 2012, Lagarde began her mandate to keep democracy's birthplace in debt bondage, assure bankers are paid, lower Greece's standard of living, impoverish its citizens, sell off all valued state assets cheap, strip mine the country of everything of worth, then replicate the process elsewhere. In other words, her job is to head the IMF's financial coup d'état against debt-entrapped sovereign states, wrecking them to pay the bankers.

Beneath Lagarde's bourgeois charm lies a financial predator chosen to pillage economies, not save them. Throughout its history, IMF policies perpetuated debt bondage, entrapping nations to service money master oligarchs, stripping sovereign nations of their independence in the process. Their peoples end up impoverished in neoserfdom if they are lucky enough to retain jobs. Lagarde's in charge to force feed austerity. She'll be well rewarded to inflict pain and suffering she'll cause, but don't expect Western media scoundrels to explain all of that.

Mandated Austerity in Greece

In his June 7, 2011 article titled, "Will Greece let EU Central Bankers Destroy Democracy,"[4] Michael Hudson discussed the proposed bailout terms. He called them "an opportunity for privatization grabs." It wasn't what local voters had bargained for with 2000 Eurozone membership. They didn't understand its unintended consequences. It included agreeing to foreign-controlled central bank authority, permitting the ECB to run Greece like a colony, substituting its will for Greek national sovereignty.

According to Professor William Black (former senior bank regulator and Savings and Loan prosecutor), Eurozone membership has strings. These include foregoing:

- the right to devalue a domestic currencies to make exports more competitive;

- sovereignty over members' own money or (for "periphery nations") influence over European Central Bank (ECB) policies;

- the right to implement expansive fiscal policies to stimulate growth.

In fact, mandated bondage "is a double oxymoron. [It prevents] effective counter-cyclical fiscal policies harm[ing] growth and stability throughout the Eurozone." Weak members hurt stronger ones. All countries lose out by spending billions on bailouts. They increase their debt and require greater amounts to service it until eventually the entire house of cards collapses.

Moreover, like all debt-entrapped countries, Greece's bailout price required structural adjustment austerity which make a bad situation worse,heaping on new penalties during hard times. Rising indebtedness results—the familiar IMF-imposed death spiral. No responsible leader should accept it.

Last year, however, in return for a $150 billion loan, Greek Prime Minister Georgios Papandreou imposed earlier cuts, including:

- large public worker layoffs;

- public sector 10% wage cuts, including a 30% reduction in salary entitlements;

- 20% cuts to civil service bonuses;

- frozen pensions;

- raising the average retirement age two years;

- higher fuel, alcohol, tobacco, and luxury goods taxes with much more to come given Greece's worsening debt problem.

Euroland officials demand multiple rounds more in return for further bailout help. Eurogroup President Jean-Claude Juncker expects nations needing help to agree, saying"In the case of countries with difficulties, it would be wise for the principal political forces of those countries to agree on the path to follow. That's what happened in Ireland, and that's what we would like to happen between the political parties in Greece," no matter the economic wreckage or human cost.

Accordingly on June 8, 2012 former Prime Minister Papandreou announced new tax increases and over $9 billion in spending cuts. Earlier he had divulged plans to raise nearly $75 billion by privatizing state enterprises, including water companies, the Piraeus and Thessalonika port facilities, the Athens racecourse, Greece's Postbank, a casino, the OPAP lottery company, and the state rail system.

He was succeeded by Lucas Papademos, a former ECB vice president, with others to follow, as the political uncertainty continues. Will the Parthenon and other national treasures be next, including the nation's soul? At year end 2011, Greek public assets were worth an estimated $440 billion. Brussels wanted at least the best of them sold, as well as assurances about debt repayment in return for continued bailout help.

However, given Greece's rising debt burden, no amount's enough. Greater austerity impedes economic growth and recovery, and deepening crisis conditions are compounded. Since 2007, Greece's economy shrank over 20% en route to exceeding 30% and total collapse. Its real debt burden exceeds $650 billion, around double the reported amount. The latest bailout deal is for about $170 billion. Its current debt exceeds what Greece can repay. Increasing it elevates crisis conditions.

Forced austerity assures harder than ever hard times. Rising unemployment exceeds 20%. Youth unemployment approaches 50%. Only a third without work get unemployment benefits. They're being slashed another 20%. There are plans for laying off another 150,000 state workers by 2015. Private sector wage cuts exceeded 20%, public sector ones around 50%. Poverty in Greece is afflicting millions. Its GDP is collapsing. So are pensions, Greece's life force, and the ability of most people to survive.

Democracy's birthplace took its last breath and died when banker-appointed prime minister Lucas Papademos (a former ECB vice president) and finance minister Evangelous Venizelos (a former Bank of Greece official) took over, exercising virtual carte blanche discretion on cuts. Parliamentarians opposing cuts are sacked. New Democracy's Antonis Samaras expelled 21 MPs, including the party's whip and shadow defense and interior ministers. PASOK's George Papandreou removed 23 opposition MPs, including former government ministers. MPs defying banker diktats don't survive.

No one's sure what's coming next. Perhaps it's tyranny under martial law, followed by new rounds of austerity cuts until Greece is bled dry and collapses. It's at the epicenter of global pillage, a symbol of how destructive money power in private hands ruthlessly pursues its interests at the public's expense. Economist Charles Wyplosz calls the austerity madness "pseudo-science," forecasting that debt default awaits Greece, Portugal, Italy and perhaps other troubled Eurozone economies. The longer they wait, the deeper the hole and greater pain.

The Argentina Solution

In December 2001, Argentina halted all debt payments to domestic and foreign creditors. Months earlier, IMF loan help had deepened the country's burden. Finally, by 2005, $100 billion in debt restructuring was completed on a take it or leave it basis. Stiff haircuts of around 65% were imposed on creditors. Most decided something was better than nothing. In 2010, the holdouts eventually capitulated, accepting similar terms. Sustained economic growth followed from 2003 through 2007. Vital debt restructuring and a devalued currency assured it.

Greece and other troubled Eurozone countries can relieve their burdens the same way, reclaiming sovereign rights by reinstating their pre-euro currencies. They never should have sacrificed them in the first place. So far, Greece's banker-controlled parliamentarians disagree. On February 12, 2012, they passed sweeping austerity measures on top of multiple previous rounds. New measures included:

- sacking 15,000 public workers in 2012 and 150,000 by 2015,

- slashing private sector wages by 20%;

- lowering monthly minimum wages from 750 to 600 euros;

- cutting fast disappearing monthly unemployment benefits from 460 to 360 euros; and

- reducing pensions many Greeks need to survive by 15%.

Another 130 billion euro bailout was secured. The more financial aid Greece gets, the greater its debt, the harder it is to repay, the more future aid is needed, and the deeper the country's economic abyss.

No matter. Troika power kleptocrats—the IMF, EU and European Central Bank (ECB)—demanded deep cuts Money power dictates that the bankers get paid first. Under crisis conditions, Greece's economy is dying. In December 2011, manufacturing plunged 15.5% year-over-year. Industrial output sank 11.3%. Unemployment topped 20%. Youth joblessness approaches 50%, and suicides doubled since economic decline began.

As a result, capital flight's increasing. People are voting with their feet and leaving. Those remaining face hospitals short of medicines, unprecedented homelessness and hunger, schools without basic supplies, and imagine what's coming when new cuts are implemented.

Moreover, bankers demand more. So far, mandated wealth confiscation alone is their only excluded diktat, but it's happening incrementally. Under systematic sacking, Greece's life force is dying in meltdown. No wonder economist Michael Hudson calls predatory finance "a form of warfare." Standing armies pale by comparison. Financial oligarchs wage war by other means and take no prisoners. They seize land, infrastructure, other tangible assets, and all material wealth. In the process, countries and ordinary people are devastated.

Greece is effectively bankrupt. Only its obituary's not written. Its people have three choices—starve, leave or rebel. Street protests and strikes produce nothing. Banker controlled parliamentarians don't care. Replacing them is crucial, by whatever means necessary. Nothing else can work, and delay only exacerbates intolerable conditions.

An Historical Analogue

Current banker-imposed policies are similar to the crushing Treaty of Versailles reparations imposed on Germany. Fascism under Hitler emerged. WW II followed. The Versailles terms were outrageous. In May 1921, Germany got an ultimatum—accept the terms within six days or face industrial Ruhr Valley military occupation. Left with no choice, it accepted. Germany's colonial possessions and raw material resources were seized.

In the end, both sides lost out. By 1929, unmanageable debt had overwhelmed world finance and monetary policy. Wall Street's crash followed. An unsustainable pyramid was built on punitive war debts. Wall Street and other major banks enforced paymentsthat exceeded America's annual 1920s foreign trade. Rebuilding and modernizing war-torn Europe was sacrificed to pay bankers.

Germany got the worst of it. Its Reichsbank had to print enormous amounts of money to survive. Catastrophic hyperinflation followed. In January 1923, the mark dropped to 18,000 to the dollar. By July, it was 353,000, in August 4,620,000, and by November an astonishing 4,200,000,000,000. It became worthless. German savings were destroyed, and calamitous events became inevitable.

Lost assets compounded economic misery. Germany's colonies became League of Nations Mandates, as Alsace-Lorraine, West Prussia, Upper Silesia and other territories were ceded to Britain, France, Belgium, Czechoslovakia, and Poland. Germany's agricultural resources were lost, along with 75% of its iron ore, 68% of zinc ore, 26% of coal, as well as Alsatian textile industries and potash mines. In addition, Germany's entire merchant fleet was taken, as well as a portion of its transport and fishing fleet, plus locomotives, railroad cars and trucks to pay war debts.

Impossible terms were imposed; 132 billion gold marks were demanded at 6% annual interest. As a result, inflation soared and German industrial activity plunged. Reichsbank and other German bank assets were seized. German marks became worthless. Public anger grew, leading to communism and fascism vying for power. In 1923, the so-called Dawes Plan (named for US banker Charles Dawes) was adopted, prioritizing the payment of the bankers. Effectively, looting was enforced which continued until 1929 when the debt pyramid collapsed.

A banking crisis followed. So did capital flight. Germany's economy crashed. The Great Depression emerged, empowering radical political elements.

The rest is history. WW II left 40 million dead and Europe in ruins. In other words, when public pain exceeds thresholds of no return, all bets are off. Often the unthinkable happens. It did before and may again now.

Don't bet against it.

ENDNOTES

1	< http://www.informationclearinghouse.info/article28431.htm>
2	< http://www.forbes.com/power-women/>
3	< http://www.globalresearch.ca/imf-regime-change-with-christine-lagarde-us-corporations-enter-the-french-government/>
4	< http://www.globalresearch.ca/will-greece-let-eu-central-bankers-destroy-democracy>

7

JPMORGAN CHASE
ON CAPITOL HILL

On June 13, 2012, JPMorgan Chase CEO Jamie Dimon testified before the Senate Banking Committee. He discussed his firm's recent trading loss and industry practices. It was more of a homecoming than grilling, since Washington is Wall Street occupied territory. Foxes guard the hen house. Regulators don't regulate. There's no oversight. Investigations rarely happen but even those conducted are whitewashed. Criminal fraud is encouraged, not curbed. You could say, it's institutionalized. Congress, the administration, the SEC, and credit rating agencies are incestuously involved with giant banks and other major financial institutions. Whatever the latter want, they get. Wall Street never had it so good. Senators didn't lay a glove on Dimon. His grand theft business model wasn't explained. Why would anybody ask him about that?

Former bank regulator/financial fraud expert Bill Black's book titled *The Best Way to Rob A Bank Is To Own One*[1] told all. He coined the term "control fraud." It lets corporate officials commit grand theft. Trillions of dollars are stolen and nothing intervenes to stop it.

On May 10, 2012 Dimon announced a $2 billion trading loss. Some estimates place it multiples higher. "Trading" is now a euphemism for speculation, with the stakes high enough to cause crises. JPMorgan is only the tip of the iceberg. Other banks are similarly deeply troubled. We'll hear about that in future announcements. Only cursory explanations will be provided. Even what Morgan bet on and lost wasn't identified.

European securities speculation looks likely. The big trader in this is called the London Whale due to the size of the credit derivatives bets he took, one of which may be as large as $100 billion. Scoundrel media reports said little about it.[2] Troubled Eurozone economies face deepening depressions. Bank problems accompany them. Investing in their sovereign and/or private debt entails great risks. Dimon attributed the loss to credit default swaps derivatives trading. They're the most widely traded derivative. They're unregulated insurance bets between two parties on whether or not a company's bonds may default.

Ellen Brown, author of *The Web of Debt*,[3] once asked: What if "the smartest guys in the room designed their credit default swaps [but] forgot to ask one thing—what if the parties on the other side of the bet don't have the money to pay up?" When crises erupt, they don't. Turmoil hits markets. Lack of oversight makes it inevitable. Bankers get bailouts. Who said crime doesn't pay? Ordinary people are hardest hit.

JP Morgan's loss relates directly to the European finance capital's crisis. It also shows how Europe's banks and America's are interconnected. Trouble on one side of the Atlantic assures it on the other. Contagion then spreads globally. In 2008, speculative excess brought down investment and commercial banks, insurers, and shadow banks. They're still troubled..

JP Morgan was considered America's most stable bank but its troubles reveal an entirely different picture. Bill Black thinks it may be "the new Fannie Mae." In 2008, Fannie Mae's subprime portfolio blew up, unraveling piece by piece. It was nationalized so taxpayers pay the tab. It remains sick on life support.

Earlier problems within the banking system remain unresolved. Nothing's been done yet to fix things. The Dodd-Frank financial reform bill, which includes the much-touted Volker rule, was signed into law in 2010 and supposed to come into force in 2012. But it left the actual provisions of the bill to be defined by the central bank and other regulators, who are hoping to finish work on the actual provisions by the end of 2012, and then will give the banks until 2014 to "make a good faith effort to comply".[4] As a result, speculative excesses continue. Some analysts think it's worse than ever. Massive balance sheet losses remain and the bailouts only conceal them. Trillions of dollars given to the banks have bought them time, nothing else.

Phony stress tests conceal the gravity of today's crisis. Mark-to-market accounting was suspended. False reporting of the actual value of bank assets followed. JPMorgan's loss was inevitable and signals much more to come.

Senators didn't hold Dimon's feet to the fire. The nationally televised hearing was more love fest than grilling. Why not, when 16 of the committee's 22 members get JPMorgan campaign cash? Anti-foreclosure protesters delayed Dimon's testimony. One shouted "Stop foreclosures." Another said "Jamie Dimon's a crook." Dimon looked unperturbed. They were hustled out of the Senate chamber handcuffed. Expect charges to follow. At the same time, Dimon's free to keep stealing and let taxpayers pay the tab if the mounting losses turn out to be too great to cover.

On June 12, 2012, Bloomberg headlined "House of Dimon Marred by CEO Complacency Over Unit's Risk,"[5] saying that Dimon treated the chief investment office (CIO) differently from other JPM departments. Rigorous scrutiny and transparency were absent. Though concerns were raised, Dimon ignored them. Why worry when big money is being made? What Dimon knew and when, he didn't say. But bear in mind: he's known as a hands-on boss. He overseas a vast financial empire. With over $2.3 trillion in assets, JPM became the largest US bank last year.

According to former Federal Reserve Bank of Minneapolis CEO Gary Stern,institutions like JPM "are too big to manage because even the bank that was considered to be the best-managed turns out to have had a significant glitch." Bloomberg called risk management at JPM's CIO a "world of its own", noting:

> This year its traders valued some of their positions at prices that differed from the investment bank, people familiar with the situation have said.
>
> One trader built up positions in credit derivatives so large and market-moving he became known as the London Whale.
>
> It was those bets on credit-default swaps known as the Markit CDX North America Investment Grade Series 9 that backfired and forced JPMorgan to disclose the trading loss.When risks got out of hand, board members lacked the experience to police them. No one on JPM's risk policy committee worked as a banker. At issue is how could Wall Street's "best run bank" operate this way? Answers weren't forthcoming.

In 2005, Bloomberg reported on JPM's risk model after it acquired Bank One. When Dimon became CEO, he created the CIO, which speculates on high-risk assets like credit default swaps and similar investments. Dimon encouraged it. Again, why worry when things go well?

Former North America CIO head David Olsen said he was told when hired: "We want to ramp up the ability to generate profits for the firm. This is Jamie's new vision for the company." Until things cratered, profits and assets surged. High-risk bets paid off. Subprime ones did handsomely.

> In addition to making speculative bets, the CIO took on a bigger role after the financial crisis, hedging JPMorgan's potential losses on loans and corporate

bonds by taking positions in credit derivatives.[6]Insiders said transparency was sorely lacking. According to "Black Swan"[7] author Nassim Taleb, JPM's "risk management is as amateurish as you can get on Wall Street." The firm "is vastly more fragile today than it was five years ago, and the system is more fragile today with more too-big-to-fail banks with proven incompetence at their management level."[8]

When Dimon announced $2 billion in trading losses last month, the CIO unit had over $100 billion in asset-backed "structured vehicles," as well as another $100 billion in credit default swaps. These types of bets contributed heavily to plunging markets in 2008. Accounting manipulation conceals the severity of the impact when they fail. The worst is yet to come out. JPM's CIO operates like a high-risk hedge fund. Taleb believes it incurs 10-15 times more risk. Losing a big bet assures trouble. Lose several or more and company solvency is threatened. Other Wall Street giants are tarnished by the same brush.

Systemically destructive strategies work as planned when things go well. Otherwise taxpayers get the bill. It's a win-win scheme. Senate banking committee members did nothing to expose it. The June 13, 2012 Senate Hearings looked more like a coronation than a crucifixion.

ENDNOTES

1   Bill Black, *The Best Way to Rob a Bank is To Own One*, University of Texas Press, 2005.

2   For a taste of how little, check out Reuters here <http://news.yahoo.com/jpmorgan-ceo-says-caught-london-whale-trades-172438058--finance.html> and Wall Street Journal here <http://blogs.wsj.com/deals/2012/10/12/london-whale-becomes-immaterial-to-j-p-morgan/>

3   <http://www.webofdebt.com/>

4   <http://www.bloomberg.com/news/2012-09-14/volcker-rule-needs-narrow-hedge-exemption-cftc-s-chilton-says.html>

5   <http://www.bloomberg.com/news/2012-09-14/volcker-rule-needs-narrow-hedge-exemption-cftc-s-chilton-says.html>

6   Ibid.

7   Nassim Taleb, The *Black Swan: The Impact of the Highly Improbable*, Random House, 2007.

8   Supra, note 5.

8

GEORGE SOROS

NEW WORLD ORDER
CONFIDENCE MAN

In July 1944, 730 delegates from 44 nations met at the Mount Washington Hotel in Bretton Woods, NH for a UN Monetary and Financial Conference. Its purpose was to establish a post-war international monetary system of convertible currencies, fixed exchange rates, free trade, with the US dollar as the world's reserve currency linked to gold, and those of other nations fixed to the dollar.

It also designed an institutional framework for market-based capital accumulation to assure newly liberated colonies would pursue capitalist economic development beneficial to the victorious allies, mainly America.

In addition, the IMF and World Bank were established to integrate developing nations into the Global North-dominated world economy. Their original missions were:

- to establish stable exchange rates linked to the dollar and bridge temporary payment imbalances (the IMF); and

- to provide credit to war-torn developing countries (the World Bank).

In actuality, these institutions served as a means of debt entrapment whereby the wealth of what were then termed "emerging markets" was transferred from developing countries to powerful Western bankers. Both bodies have proved hugely exploitive, as is their purpose to this day.

The scheme obligates indebted nations to take new loans to service old ones. While many caught on to the trap, paid out their loans and sought to avoid new ones, worsening financial conditions are propelling many countries back into the maw of the IMF once again, even though this time they know better. Once again the process assures rising indebtedness and imposes structural adjustment-based austerity, including:

- privatization of state enterprises;

- mass layoffs;

- deregulation;

- deep social spending cuts;

- wage freezes or cuts;

- unrestricted free market access for western corporations;

- corporate-friendly tax cuts;

- crackdowns on or elimination of trade unionism; and

- harsh repression against those opposing a system incompatible with social democracy.

Overall, since WW II, a significant degree of what was once public wealth was shifted into powerful private hands. As the gap between super-rich elites and working households widens,the process is becoming more intensely predatory than ever, and the amounts involved are skyrocketing.

In 1971, the system unraveled when Nixon closed the gold window, ending the last link between gold, the dollar, and sound money. Thereafter, currencies floated, competing with each other in a casino-like environment. As a result, powerful insiders manipulate the process fraudulently. They include hedge funds, giant international banks, and governments, at times cooperatively with others in their own mutual self-interest. George Soros is a player, very much a major one. More on that, below.

In his book *Super Imperialism: The Economic Strategy of American Empire* and other writings, Michael Hudson explained: :

- how the dollar glut finances US imperialism and corporate interests by circulating surplus dollars globally to further financial speculation and corporate takeovers;

- how global central banks "recyle these dollar inflows (into) US Treasury bonds to finance the federal US budget deficit; and most important the military character of the US payments deficit and the domestic federal budget deficit."

In other words, the central bank's printing dollars finances US corporate takeovers and speculative excesses. These, in turn, create bubbles and global economic crises, as well as facilitate America's reckless spending, militarism, and imperial wars, enabling the establishment of hundreds of bases worldwide, and American projection overall of belligerence and exploitation at the expense of democratic values and social justice.

Sooner or later, however, excesses erode confidence and produce change. It's especially so today with the Federal Reserve sacrificing the dollar's dwindling strength to bail out Wall Street at the expense of productive economic growth and stability.

The more dollar strength and safety erode, the less likely foreign investors will tolerate buying bad dollar-denominated assets whose value is likely to decline further over time. For decades, the sale of US Treasuries has given America a free lunch to finance counterproductive policy.

Hudson sees international tensions growing for the next generation because of America's reckless monetarism, perpetual wars, and extreme wealth gap between super-rich elites and ordinary people.

For decades, US companies had a competitive advantage stemming from the Washington Consensus policy prescriptions and the Bretton Woods institutions the US controls.

They've afforded America a free lunch to rule by forcing other countries into debt bondage, and threatening to bring down the global monetary system if enough of them balk. Where financial warfare fails to intimidate, the military is sent in to do the job. So far financial domination mostly succeeds because Europe and Asia lack the political will to establish a new international economic order. They let America reap their wealth to reinforce its "new kind of centralized global planning" based on financialization and a US Treasury securities standard.

In WTO terms, this system transfers foreign trade gains from other economies back to America by way of dollar deposits in Treasuries. It drains their resources overall, and promotes their dependency, locking them in to the lower end of production chains, rather than promoting self-sufficiency. It's backed up with hard line militarism and threats of systemic monetary collapse.

Eventually, exploited countries balk when faced with "taxation without representation," a "quid without quo," and the free lunch enjoyed by "the world's payments-surplus nations."

The longer America demands this tribute by glutting the world's economies with dollars, the more likely disadvantaged nations will object, and eventually perhaps withdraw from the IMF, World Bank and WTO altogether.

Globalists like George Soros aim to exploit that possibility, among other ways through Bretton Woods 2.0 to develop ideas and policies for a new financial world order that elitists like himself will control.

George Soros—Predatory Billionaire Investor

Soros' rogue investing is notorious. For example, in 1992, he made a billion dollars sabotaging European monetary policy by attacking the European Rate Mechanism (ERM) through a highly leveraged speculative assault on the British pound. As a result, he forced its devaluation and the ERM breakup.

In June 2003, Neil Clark wrote a *New Statesman* article explaining Soros' machinations as a rogue predator—how he "made billions out of the Far Eastern currency crash of 1997," and was fined in 2002 "for insider trading by a court in France."[1] When asked about the turmoil his speculation caused, Soros dismissively said: "As a market participant, I don't need to be concerned with the consequences of my actions."

While earning billions from rogue investing, he's caused havoc for millions globally. More still by his International Crisis Group and Open Society (open meaning for him to plunder) collaboration with Zbigniew Brzezinski, Al Gore, General Wesley Clark, Richard Perle, Paul Wolfowitz, and many other notorious scoundrels and organizations.

For decades, Soros operated roguishly for a buck. For example, in 1998, he wrote an outrageous letter to Bill Clinton, calling for a "comprehensive political and military strategy for bringing down Saddam Hussein and his regime" for reasons that the Bush administration would subsequently endorse. He's also connected to the Carlyle Group that profits handsomely from defense contracts related to militarism and imperial wars.

There his partners and associates include G.H.W. Bush, James Baker, Colin Powell, former UK Prime Minister John Major, Frank Carlucci, Richard Darman, at one time bin Laden family members, and many other well-connected figures.

Clark explained that Soros "may not, as sometimes suggested, be a fully paid-up CIA agent. But that his corporations and NGOs are closely wrapped up in US expansionism cannot seriously be doubted."

He turned on Bush II over tactics, not ideology—for committing the cardinal sin of giving away the game through overzealously endorsing belligerence.

In fact, Soros strongly supports financial and military warfare for greater profits globally, to gain control over money, resources and markets. But he wants it done skillfully with little notice. It's his quiet way. Accordingly, he uses wealth and influence to oust "bad for business" regimes. For example, Clark said, he was instrumental in the Soviet collapse by:

> distribut(ing) $3 million a year to dissidents including Poland's solidarity movement, Charter 77 in Czechoslovakia, and Andrei Sakharov in the Soviet Union. In 1984, he founded his first Open Society Institute in Hungary and pumped millions of dollars into opposition movements and independent media. Ostensibly aimed at building up a 'civil society,' these initiatives were designed to weaken the existing political structures and pave the way for eastern Europe's eventual exploitation by global capital.Soros now takes credit for the "Americanization of eastern Europe" by exploiting its wealth and people for profit.

In Yugoslavia, Clark said:

> The Yugoslavs remained stubbornly resistant and repeatedly returned Slobodan Milosevic's reformed Socialist Party to government. Soros was equal to the challenge.
>
> From 1991, his Open Society Institute channeled more than $100 million to [anti-Milosevic elements] funding political parties, publishing houses and 'independent' media [like Radio B92].

When Washington ousted Milosevic in 2000, "all that was left was to cart [him] to the Hague tribunal, co-financed by Soros" and other so-called human rights custodians. Today, Yugoslavia is balkanized, its people exploited, and Kosovar-governed by Prime Minister Hashim Thaci, a Washington-supported unindicted drug trafficker with known organized crimes ties.

Soros, however, profited hugely. He's done so, in fact, in each country he targeted at the expense of freedom, democratic values, and public welfare.

> In Kosovo, for example, he invested $50 million in an attempt to gain control of the Trepca mine complex, where there are vast reserves of gold, silver, lead and

other minerals estimated to be worth [about] $5 billion.
He thus copied a pattern he [used] to great effect over
the whole of eastern Europe [through] 'shock therapy'
and 'economic reform,' then swooping in with his
associates to buy valuable state assets at knock-down
prices.In fact, his Pax Americana strategy differs only
from Bush II in subtlety. "But it is just as ambitious
and just as deadly," whether forwarded by military or
financial warfare for maximum profits.

Soros' Institute for New Economic Thinking (INET) Bretton Woods Conference

From April 8-11, 2011 INET's second annual conference
addressed global economic crisis aftershocks, as part of a wide-ranging
effort to "engage the larger European Union, as well as emerging
economies of Eastern Europe, Latin America and Asia" to accept Soros'
New World Order ideas.

Directed to "inspir[e] and provok[e] new economic thinking,"
over 200 academics, business and government leaders (many with direct
ties to him) attended.

They included INET's Soros and Robert Johnson, former UK
Prime Minister Gordon Brown, Paul Volker, Larry Summers, Joseph
Stiglitz, Kenneth Rogoff, Jeffrey Sachs (whose shock therapy poison
wrecked post-Soviet Russia and Eastern Europe), Carmen Reinhart from
the [Pete] Peterson Institute for International Economics, the Bank of
England's Andy Haldane, Henry Kaufman, and other New World Order
elites.

They came to plot new ways for global financial control, plunder
and profits. Topics discussed included:

- The emerging economic and political order: what lies ahead?

- Bretton Woods: what can we learn from the past in designing
the future?

- Getting back on track: macroeconomic management after a
financial crisis.

- Sovereignty and institutional design in the global age: the global
market and the nation states.

- Can sovereignty and effective international supervision be reconciled: the challenge of large complex financial institutions.

- Exploring complexity in economic theory.

- The political economy of structural adjustment: understanding the obstacles to cooperation.

- The market or the state: can market forces deliver innovation, education, and infrastructure?

- Sustainable economic systems.

- Optimal currency areas and governance: the challenge of Europe.

- The architecture of Asia: financial structure and an emerging economic system, and

- Rising to the challenge: equity, adjustment and balance in the world economy.

A Final Comment

Globalist Soros believes the American empire should be replaced by world government with a global currency under UN rule. In other words, he wants national sovereignty replaced by centralized control over money, populations, resources and markets. If established, it would be an undemocratic ruler-serf society unfit to live in except for leaders and profiteers.

On January 25, 2010, *New York Times* writer Andrew Sorkin headlined, "Still Needed: A Sheriff of Finance," quoting Soros as saying ahead of the 2008 World Economic Forum in Davos, Switzerland: "We need a global sheriff"

Perhaps he has himself in mind.

ENDNOTES

1   <http://www.mindfully.org/WTO/2003/George-Soros Statesman 2jun 03.htm>

9

GOLDMAN SACHS

MAKING MONEY
BY STEALING IT

Money power in private hands and democracy can't co-exist. Wall Street crooks have transformed America into an unprecedented money making racket.

Goldman Sachs symbolizes Master of the Universe manipulative fraud. It's been involved in nearly all financial scandals since the 19th century. It makes money the old-fashioned way. It steals it through fraud, grand theft, market front-running and manipulation, scamming investors, bribing political Washington, installing its executives in top administration posts, and getting open-ended low or no interest bailouts when needed. Its business model and culture assure billions of bonus dollars for company officials, complicit traders, and others on the take. It's more like a crime family than a bank. It's part of a coterie of others like it on Wall Street that includes corrupt politicians.

Compared to Goldman, Bernie Madoff was small-time. So are most other swindlers. Those who matter sit in Wall Street board rooms, plotting other scams. Bill Black, former bank regulator expert on white-collar crime, public finance, economics, and related law, explained Goldman shenanigans pertaining to earlier SEC charges this way:

> Goldman designed a rigged trifecta. It turned a massive loss into a material profit by selling deeply underwater, toxic CDOs it owned. It helped make John Paulson (CEO of a huge hedge fund that Goldman would love to have as an ally) a massive profit—in a 'profession' where reciprocal favors are key, and blew up its customers that purchased the CDOs.[1]

An SEC civil suit charged Goldman with defrauding customers. Goldman had made billions, and the suit was settled for $550 million— pocket change, the equivalent of four 2009 revenue days. It hardly mattered. No executive was fined or imprisoned.

Grand theft continues unabated. It includes fraudulent pump-and-dump schemes. Major media scoundrels don't explain what is going on to the public. Only the scammed customers and the insiders complicit in the dirty game understand.

On March 4, 2012, Bill Black used James Q. Wilson's "broken windows" metaphor pertaining to blue collar crime, applying it to far more serious elite white-collar offenses. But none rise to the level of financial crimes. The amounts involved and the degree of destruction are staggering. Broken lives, communities, and economies result. The landscape's littered with them.

No firm is more adept at amassing fraudulent fortunes than Goldman. With stupefying arrogance, its CEO, Lloyd Blankfein, calls what he does "doing God's work." But what's worse is to see the Supreme Court rulings make banks and other financial entities immune from charges of securities fraud by those they have harmed. Only Washington may sue for redress.

It's also appalling that Murdoch's *Wall Street Journal* "serve[s] as cheerleader and apologist for those" who amass wealth by stealing it, said Black.

Goldman Executive Resigns

Broken clocks are right twice a day. On March 14, so was *The New York Times*. It gave rare op-ed space to high level Goldman executive Greg Smith for views worth sharing. He served as executive director and head of the firm's domestic equity derivatives business in Europe, the Middle East and Africa. Headlining, "Why I Am Leaving Goldman Sachs,"[2] Smith wrote that after almost 12 years with the firm, today was his last day. He had worked there "long enough to understand the trajectory of its culture, its people and its identity. And I can honestly say that the environment now is as toxic and destructive as I have ever seen it."

In "simplest terms," he said client interests are sidelined. Goldman thinks only about making money. "The firm has veered so far from the place I joined right out of college that I can no longer in good conscience say that I identify with what it stands for."

In less blunt terms than Black, this writer, and other critics, Smithe stopped short of labeling its grand theft model as such, but comments he made suggested it. An earlier Goldman culture contributed to its success, he said. "It revolved around teamwork, integrity, a spirit of humility, and always doing right by our clients."

Exaggerated? According to Smith, "virtually no trace" of what he admired remains. Whatever pride he once had is now gone. It was time to leave when he no longer could look aspiring students wanting Goldman jobs "in the eye and tell them what a great place this was to work."

How can Goldman be operating like a crime family? Simple. Its business model involves grand theft. Customers are defrauded, not helped. Politicians are bought like toothpaste. Laws are subverted and ignored. Others are discarded or rewritten at its behest. Entire economies are wrecked for profit.

When future Goldman histories are written, Smith said, honest ones will say Blankfein, president Gary Cohn, and other top executives "lost hold of the firm's culture on their watch. I truly believe that this decline in the firm's moral fiber represents the single most serious threat to its long-run survival."

Smith said his career involved advising two of the largest global hedge funds, five of America's largest asset managers, and three of the Middle East's most prominent sovereign wealth funds. His clients manage over a trillion dollars in assets.

He took pride in advising them "to do what I believe is right for them, even if it means less money for the firm. This view is becoming increasingly unpopular at Goldman Sachs." He knew it was time to leave. "Leadership used to be about ideas, setting an example and doing the right thing. Today, if you make enough money for the firm (and are not currently an ax murderer), you will be promoted into a position of influence."

Three key ways to make that money:

(1) Advise clients to invest in assets Goldman wants to dump, including toxic ones.

(2) Get clients to buy what makes Goldman most money.

(3) Trade "any illiquid, opaque product with a three-letter acronym," no matter how toxic or without merit.

Smith attended sales meetings devoid of seeking ways to help Goldman clients. Instead the focus was on maximizing Goldman's profit, no matter how illegally. "It makes me ill," he said, "how callously people talk about ripping their clients off. Over the last 12 months, I have seen five different managing directors refer to their own clients as 'muppets.'"

The firm's own clients are marks to be manipulated and scammed for profit. Smith can't explain why senior managers don't understand that losing client trust means forfeiting their business, no matter if you're the smartest guys in the room. They'll know you're smart enough to scam them without having to hear back room insults about "muppets," "ripping eyeballs out," and "getting paid" at their expense. He hopes his article "can be a wake-up call " to Goldman's board. "Make the client the focal point of your business again. Without clients you will not make money. In fact, you will not exist."

"Weed out the morally bankrupt people, no matter how much money they make for the firm." Make "people want to work here for the right reasons. People who care only about making money will not sustain this firm—or the trust of its clients—for very much longer."

A Final Comment

Goldman's entire history, or at least most of it, reflects predation. Its scams pre-date Smith's birth. In the 1920s, its Ponzi scheme investment trusts defrauded investors. Goldman profited. They lost out, and when Wall Street crashed, they were left high, dry, and broke.

One trust sold to investors reflected standard Goldman practice in relation to others. Its offering price was $104 a share. It soon became virtually worthless at $1.75, losing over 98% of its value. Unwary buyers then and now lose out. Only the stakes keep on getting bigger.

Today the stakes are enormous. Getting in bed with Goldman is like swimming with sharks. You're prey. They're predators. Those burned understand Goldman's culture enough to know it's toxic and corrupted.

In 2002, Goldman was largely responsible for Greece's debt problems, assisting government borrowers in circumventing Eurozone rules in return for mortgaging assets.

Using creative accounting, the debt was hidden through off-balance sheet shenanigans. Derivatives called cross-currency swaps were used. Government debt was issued in dollars and yen was swapped for euros, then later exchanged back to the original currencies.

Debt entrapment followed. Greece was held hostage to repay it, leaving the country raped and pillaged. Paying bankers comes first. Doing it has left Greeks impoverished, high and dry. Goldman profited enormously by scamming an entire country and its innocent millions who had nothing to do with that first dirty deal. Its business model thrives on re-enacting similar schemes globally. It's about profits, no matter the huge cost to others. Expecting this leopard to change spots is like imagining reformers will transform Washington.

Former alderman Paddy Bauler once said "Chicago ain't ready for reform." It's still not ready and may never be.

Neither is political Washington, Goldman, other Wall Street crooks, or their counterparts throughout corporate America. They connive, cheat, profiteer from wars, drain trillions from households and the national treasury, wage war on labor, sell dangerous products, destroy the environment, and do whatever they damn well please, complicit with corrupt politicians who let them.

Goldman and other Wall Street giants are the worst of the lot. Standing armies pale by comparison. Michael Hudson calls finance warfare by other means. Generalissimo bankers run everything. Their modus operandi is pillaging households, investors, communities, and countries for profit.

They're holding humanity hostage. It's up to public rage to change things.

ENDNOTES

1   <http://www.nextnewdeal.net/bill-black-interview-great-global-bank-robbery-part-2>
2   <http://www.nytimes.com/2012/03/14/opinion/why-i-am-leaving-goldman-sachs.html?_r=2>

10

A BIG WIN FOR PREDATORY HEALTH CARE GIANTS

Voting 5-4 on June 28, 2012 on *National Federation of Independent Business, et al. v. Sebelius, Secretary of Health and Human Services, et al.*, the Supreme Court upheld what should have been rejected: the right of Congress to enact most provisions of the *Patient Protection and Affordable Care Act (PPACA)*, a.k.a. Obamacare.

Pro-business High Court rulings aren't new. Since the 19th century, what business wants matters most. *Santa Clara County v. Southern Pacific Railway* stands out. It granted corporations legal personhood. Ever since, corporations have had people rights without responsibilities. Their limited liability status exempts them from that. As a result, they've profited hugely and continue winning favorable high and lower court rulings.

From March 26-28, 2012, oral arguments on PPACA's constitutionality were heard. Contentious issues included:

- mandating that all adults acquire health insurance or be taxed to compensate;

- PPACA's Medicaid expansion provisions;

- whether the Anti-Injunction Act bars courts from reviewing the individual mandate until it's effective in January 2014; and

- "severability:" namely, whether one issue can be struck down while leaving others intact.

Many PPACA provisions took effect. Key ones, including the individual mandate, are to begin in January 2014.

Twenty-six states sued to overturn Obamacare. The Supreme Court heard the Florida case, including the others as plaintiffs. A record pro and con 136 amicus briefs ("friends of the court") were filed for Court consideration.

In 2010, Ralph Nader called Obamacare a boon to predatory giants who stood to profit hugely, at the expense of ordinary people. Nader called PPACA "a pay-or-die system that's the disgrace of the Western world."

Wendell Potter, former vice president of CIGNA, a global health insurance company, said Obamacare shifts costs to consumers, offers inadequate or unaffordable access, forces Americans to pay higher deductibles for less coverage, and ends up scamming them.

Physicians for a National Health Program (PNHP) headlined their press release " 'Health law upheld, but health needs still unmet:' national doctors group," saying that modest PPACA benefits don't remedy "our health care crisis." The unresolved Obamacare issues include:

- exclusion of a public option and universal coverage;

- the millions left uninsured;

- many more underinsured;

- unaffordability for most people "because of high co-pays and gaps in coverage that leave patients vulnerable to financial ruin in the event of serious illness;" and

- rising predatory costs.

Obamacare's empowering of private insurers Is highly contentious. They "siphon off hundreds of billions of health care dollars for overhead, profit and the paperwork demands from doctors and hospitals." The bottom line priorities of the insurance companies effectively deny care by making it unaffordable for millions. They and other industry giants obstruct reform out of antipathy towards the setting of public welfare-oriented (socialist) precedents.

In contrast, universal coverage assures comprehensive affordable care. Predatory middlemen are excluded. Doing so would save $400 billion annually. Using that money for care instead of for corporate profits makes it possible to cover everyone.

Comparable state plans have failed. Residents were betrayed.

Their so-called reforms "founder[ed] on the shoals of skyrocketing costs, even as the private insurers have continued to amass vast fortunes."

Medicare for all offers real reform. Everyone in. No one out. Healthcare is a universal right. Free societies should never tolerate commodifying a universal right. Reform efforts have never succeeded. Lobby power blocked them. In 1917, 15 states introduced a standard health insurance bill. Eight others established commissions to study the issue. But the proposals were weak and confusing. They were dead on arrival. In the 1930 and 1940s, government-sponsored health insurance resurfaced. The issue remained contentious. Industry giants again blocked change.

Post-war, employer-provided coverage increased but retirees, the disabled, unemployed, and others were left uninsured. After years of debate, Medicare and Medicare included them.

Nonetheless, efforts to cover everyone affordably failed. PPACA is only the latest example. It's a rationing scheme to enrich insurers, drug companies and large hospital chains. PNHP speaks for millions when it says:

> What is truly unrealistic is believing that we can provide universal and affordable health care in a system dominated by private insurers and Big Pharma.
> The American people desperately need a universal health system that delivers comprehensive, equitable, compassionate and high-quality care, with free choice of provider and no financial barriers to access.

Convoluted arguments upheld PPACA's controversial individual mandate provision that requires purchasing coverage from private insurers. Ruling with the majority, Chief Justice John Roberts said:

> The Affordable Care Act's requirement that certain individuals pay a financial penalty for not obtaining health insurance may reasonably be characterized as a tax. Because the Constitution permits such a tax, it is not our role to forbid it, or to pass upon its wisdom or fairness...
> The federal government does have the power to impose a tax on those without health insurance.[1]

Roberts added that he and other majority justices abstained on judging whether passing PPACA was right or wrong. "Those decisions are entrusted to our nation's elected leaders, who can be thrown out of office if the people disagree with them," he said. "It is not our job to protect the people from the consequences of their political choices."

Supreme Court Justices Scalia, Kennedy and Alito disagreed. Their dissenting opinion called the law an affront to individual liberty that should have been entirely rejected.

> The values that should have determined our course today are caution, minimalism and the understanding that the federal government is one of limited powers but the court's ruling undermines those values at every turn.[2]

At the same time, the majority justices rejected the administration's main argument about congressional authorization to regulate interstate commerce. The Commerce Clause doesn't give legislators the right to require people buy health insurance, they said. It's "not a general license to regulate an individual from cradle to grave, simply because he will predictably engage in particular transactions,"[3] said Roberts. Albeit supporting the ruling, in a separate opinion, Justice Ruth Bader Ginsburg called arguments against the Commerce Clause "stunningly retrogressive," reflecting pre-New Deal rulings "in which the Court routinely thwarted Congress' efforts to regulate the national economy in the interest of those who labor to sustain it."[4]

The ruling limited Medicaid's expansion, restricting congressional authority to pass social welfare laws. Seven justices said Congress exceeded its constitutional authority to coerce states to participate by threatening to cut off federal funds. They can opt out of Medicaid's expansion if they wish.

When people opt out, however, it undermines efforts to cover individuals under age 65 with incomes of 133% above poverty or less, affecting around 11 million Medicaid recipients who already receive minimal care. Experts say America's poorest are left in "no-man's land." They won't be covered by federal benefits and will be ineligible for subsidized insurance.

PPACA provides 100% of the funds to expand Medicaid until 2016. Thereafter, it's 90%. The Act has made planned cuts easier. Until now, federal funding required state participation. No longer. Millions will be harmed. Many will be left out entirely. Medicaid expansion provided coverage for around 17 million Americans by 2019. States now can opt out at their discretion.

Matt Solo, executive director of the National Association of Medicaid Directors said states have a major decision to make. "There is a real debate here where states are going to have to weigh leaving huge amounts of federal dollars on the table versus accepting potential exposure in the future. Before, you just had to just hold your nose and do it,"[5] he said. He's not sure what states will do. He called the Court decision "a total surprise." It will greatly impact PPACA's future, he believes.

According to Sara Rosenbaum, professor of health law at Georgetown University, "The practical effect... will make the Medicaid expansions go more slowly."[6]

Future court decisions may have to distinguish between new programs or additions to existing ones. But for budget strapped states seeking new ways to cut costs, this ruling adds leverage. It lets them do it on the backs of those residents most needing help.

UCLA Professor of Law Adam Winkler said:

> It will be interesting to see what happens in the 26 states that challenged Obamacare. Will they go through with their threats of not expanding their own Medicaid coverage? Or will the promise of federal money persuade them to expand coverage?[7]

Opting in assures full federal coverage for three years. At the same time, Congress plans major Medicare, Medicaid, Social Security, disability, education, and other social benefits cuts post-election.

Both parties have agreed. It's part of an earlier struck "grand bargain" no matter which party controls the White House and/or Congress. Regardless of how the High Court ruled, you can expect bipartisan congressional support to inflict the most harm. Social America is fast eroding. Party leaders plan to end it entirely.

ENDNOTES

1   Syllabus, Supreme Court of the United States, National Federation of Independent Business et al. v. Sebelius, Secretary of Health and Human Services, et al., p. 44 < http://www.supremecourt.gov/opinions/11pdf/11-393c3a2.pdf>

2   Id, p. 65.

3   Id. P. 26.

4   Id., p. 2.

5   < http://www.washingtonpost.com/blogs/ezra-klein/wp/2012/06/28/

the-supreme-court-surprise-medicaid-ruling-could-reduce-coverage/?print=1>
6   < http://tpmdc.talkingpointsmemo.com/2012/06/supreme-court-health-care-medicaid-expansion-obamacare.php>
7   Id.

11

DEBT CEILING ROULETTE

In this game, the house always wins. Bipartisan complicity has stacked the deck against millions of working households. They need to know that political Washington is complicit with the corporate crooks that scam them.

The end result is the banana republicanization of America. American writer O. Henry (William Sydney Porter: 1862-1910) coined this term (to refer to his fictional Republic of Anchuria) in his book, *Cabbages and Kings*.

It refers to a politically unstable and/or repressive country where a small percentage of the population has a disproportionate share of the wealth and power—where ordinary people are exploited, often persecuted, and profits are privatized while working households bear oppressive debt burdens.

It's also a kleptocracy run by criminals in government, complicit with corporate thieves who bribe them to get their way. It's corrupt, rotten to the core gangsterism, run for personal, private gain. Both sides profit at the public's expense.

This is going on in plain sight in Washington, now a heart of darkness where bipartisan crooks are destroying personal freedoms, democratic values, and general welfare to grab everything for themselves and their corporate partners.

Obama was made president to play ball; they needed a Democrat to do what no Republican would dare. At the same time as he does it, he duplicitously claims populist credentials.

As president, Obama has been as hardline as a neocon, reflective of the ideology of the Democrat Leadership Council (DLC) that he has been pushing. The DLC has been around since the mid-1980s until operations ended early this year–perhaps because too many people caught on to its scam.

Ralph Nader called it "corporatist (and) soulless," and Obama fits the mold. He's anti-populist, anti-labor, anti-welfare, pro-business, while at the same time militaristic and pro-war seeking to ensure unchallengeable US world dominance. Nader explained that:

> To the DLC mind, Democrats are catering to 'special interests' when they [pretend to] stand up for trade unions, regulatory consumer-investor protections, a preemptive peace policy overseas, pruning the bloated military budget now devouring [the federal budget], defending Social Security from Wall Street schemes, and pressing for universal health care coverage.
>
> So right-wing is the DLC... that even opposing Bush's tax cuts for the wealthy... is considered ultra-liberal and contrary to winning campaigns. DLC ideology is indistinguishable from Republican extremism. It opposes rights for Blacks, Hispanics, Latino immigrants, Muslims, labor, the poor, consumer protections, populism, progressivism, environmental protection, peace and those for it, prosecuting corporate criminals, honest elections, and democratic governance.

There is a bipartisan cancer destroying America. Obama was made point man in charge because who would imagine he'd dare to front such injustice as America's first Black president.

In actuality, he was chosen for his commitment to wealth, power, global dominance, imperial wars, and grand theft at the expense of working Americans and ordinary people everywhere.

In July 2009, Kevin Baker's *Harper's* article headlined, "Barack Hoover Obama: The best and brightest blow it again," saying: "Three months into his presidency," it's hard to imagine the unthinkable—that Obama will fail because he won't "seize the radical moment" to change a broken system responsibly.

Even then, some observers ludicrously compared him to Franklin Roosevelt. A better comparison is Herbert Hoover who faced similar problems, though doing so isn't fair.

Hoover at least tried some ways to confront the great crisis, if inadequately. He established national voluntary initiatives to create jobs, provide charity, and create a private banking pool, but failed. He also set up a dozen Home Loan Discount Banks to help people refinance mortgages and save homes. In 1932, he established the Reconstruction Finance Corporation (RFC). It was capitalized with $500 million and authorization to borrow another $1.5 billion. In its first six months, it loaned banks over $800 million to no effect. Like today, they were retaining reserves and shunned lending. Moreover, public trust was absent because political leadership lacked courage to do more. They were hidebound by ways no longer working. Despite understanding the problem, Hoover failed because he was part of a broken system he wouldn't change.

But Roosevelt streamlined the RFC's bureaucracy. He increased its funding to recapitalize troubled banks and corporations. He confronted the crisis aggressively in the first 100 days, enacting 15 landmark laws and founding new agencies: The Bank Act of 1933 (Glass-Steagall) was enacted, separating commercial from investment banks and insurance companies, among other provisions.

- The RFC was streamlined with more capitalization and other measures to restore public trust.

- New agencies like the Home Owners Loan Corporation, Farm Credit Administration, Rural Electrification Administration, Public Works Administration, and others were funded, as well as emergency relief loans to states–something Hoover never ever did, let alone establish these New Deal policies.

- The Securities and Exchange Act of 1933. It required offers and sales of securities be registered, pursuant to the Constitution's interstate commerce clause. Along with the 1934 SEC Act, it was to enforce federal securities laws, the securities industry, the nation's financial and options exchanges, and other electronic securities markets.

Today's shenanigans were unknown in the 1930s, including derivatives and other forms of speculation now commonplace, were unknown in the 1930s.

The SEC was also charged with uncovering wrongdoing to assure investors weren't swindled, and to keep financial markets free from fraud. While its fulfillment fell far short of its promise, at least it tried.

- The Home Owners' Loan Corporation (HOLC) to refinance homes and prevent foreclosures.

- The Civilian Conservation Corps (CCC) created jobs by building roads, bridges, dams, state parks, planting trees, and various forestry and recreational programs for the Forest Service, National Park Service, Fish and Wildlife Service, Bureau of Reclamation, Bureau of Land Management, and Soil

Conservation Service.

- The Civilian Works Administration (CWA) funded states to reduce unemployment.

- The National Industrial Recovery Act (NIRA), established the National Recovery Administration to revive economic growth, encourage collective bargaining, set maximum work hours, minimum wages, at times prices, and forbid child labor in industry.

- The Public Works Administration also established projects to provide jobs, increase purchasing power, improve public welfare, and help revive economic growth.

- The Works Progress Administration (WPA) did the same, becomng the largest New Deal agency. It employed millions in every state, especially in rural and western areas.

- The Tennessee Valley Authority (TVA) provided navigation, flood control, electricity generation, and economic development. It also promoted agriculture in the depression-impacted Tennessee Valley area, covering most of Tennessee and parts of Alabama, Mississippi, Kentucky, Georgia, North Carolina, and Virginia.

- The Agricultural Adjustment Act (AAA) –though this fell short by restricting production by paying farmers to reduce and/or destroy crops and kill livestock at a time millions were impoverished and hungry. The idea was to decrease supply and raise prices but it was implemented at the worst possible time.

- The Farm Credit Act of 1933 helped farmers refinance mortgages over an extended time at below-market rates, and by so doing, helped them stay solvent and survive.

- The May 1933 Emergency Farm Mortgage Act,established during the Dust Bowl period, provided refinancing help for farmers facing foreclosure.

Despite its flaws and failures, FDR's New Deal accomplished much. It helped people, put millions back to work, and reinvigorated the national spirit. It built or renovated 700,000 miles of roads, 7,800 bridges,

45,000 schools, 2,500 hospitals, 13,000 parks and playgrounds, 1,000 airfields, and various other infrastructure, including much of Chicago's lakefront. It also cut unemployment from 25% in May 1933 to 11% in 1937.

However, (because victory was declared too early), unemployment spiked to 19% in 1938 before early war production revived economic growth, sending it lower, while heading America for full wartime employment.

Later came the *Wagner Act*. For the first time, labor was legally enabled to bargain collectively on equal terms with management. Today such a possibility has been entirely lost.

The 1935 *Social Security Act* was to this day the single most important federal program responsible for keeping seniors and others eligible out of poverty. Obama plans to gut it, perhaps first by privatization. Bush tried doing it but had failed.

Unemployment insurance was instituted in partnership with states. By 1935, nearly all the unemployed received social benefit payments.

The so-called "Soak the Rich" *Revenue Acts* of 1934 and 1935 made high income earners pay their fair share. In contrast, Obama policies favor America's super-rich at the expense of working Americans and the poor.

The Revenue Act of 1936 established an "undistributed profits tax" on corporations. Today, profitable corporations pay minimal taxes. Many get large rebates. Yet Obama wants even lower taxes. *The Revenue Act of 1937* cracked down on tax evasion. Today, it's practically de rigueur along with sanctioned speculative excesses and grand theft.

A minimum wage, 40-hour week, and time-and-a-half for overtime were guaranteed under the 1938 *Fair Labor Standards Act* (FLSA). Labor rights today are being eviscerated and lost. Obama's as committed to that as Bush and congressional hardliners were.

Roosevelt also established other initiatives to reform a broken system, put people back to work, and revive the sick economy. Nonetheless, it didn't happen until WW II because much more was needed, including incentives for business to invest.

Under Obama, however, corporate crooks take the money and run. They reward themselves with generous bonuses, stock options and benefits, investing some abroad, and stashing more in offshore tax havens.

Moreover, Obama wants all New Deal/Great Society programs gutted, which will return American to 19th century harshness. George Bernard Shaw might have had him in mind when he said: "Democracy (especially American-style) is a form of government that substitutes election by the incompetent many for the appointment of the corrupt few."

Promising change, Obama has broken every key campaign pledge he made. He conspired with Wall Street, war profiteers, and other corporate crooks to loot the nation's wealth irrespective of whether that would wreck the economy, and consign growing millions to impoverishment without jobs, homes, savings, social services, or futures.

His legacy is shameful. He betrayed the public trust, ravaged the world one country at a time, presided over a bogus democracy under a homeland security police state apparatus, and initiated the destruction of America's social contract.

In fact, he's done the impossible: governing to the right of George W. Bush.

It was clear before he took office. His economic dream team appointees included Trilateralist Paul Volker, Geitner at Treasury, Fed chairman Bernanke, and Larry Summers, responsible for financial market deregulation and massive fraud under Clinton. Others were also chosen for their fealty to wealth and power.

No wonder James Petras called him "the greatest con-man in recent history."[1] Perhaps he's the greatest ever, given the stakes.

ENDNOTES

1 James Petras, *Global Depression and Regional Wars*, Clarity Press, Inc., 2010, pp. 49-56.

12

MONEY PRINTING MADNESS

According to an ancient proverb, "Those whom the gods wish to destroy they first make mad." Perhaps it had central bankers in mind. In fall 2007, economic crisis conditions erupted. Counterproductive policies followed. Responsible measures weren't adopted and everything done so far has failed. Money printing madness has been substituted for stimulative growth policies. Since early September 2012, coordinated central bank intervention has repeated policies that haven't before worked.

For most people, conditions are much worse now than earlier. Troubled European economies are cratering As force-fed austerity cripples them. Stronger economies are faltering. Unemployment and poverty are increasing. So is public anger. According to John Williams:

> Consumers simply cannot make ends meet. Inflation-adjusted, or real, median household income declined for the fourth-straight year, plunging to its lowest level since 1995.Deflated by the CPI-U, the 2011 reading actually stood below levels seen in the late-1960s and early-1970s.
>
> At the same time, despite the ongoing nature of the economic and systemic-solvency crises, and the effects of the 2008 financial panic, income dispersion—the movement of income away from the middle towards both high- and low-level extremes—has hit a record high, instead of moderating, as might be expected during periods of financial distress. Extremes in income dispersion usually foreshadow financial-market and economic calamities. With the current circumstance at

a record extreme, and well above levels estimated to
have prevailed before the 1929 stock-market crash and
the Great Depression, increasingly difficult times are
likely for the next several years.[1]

Economist Paul Craig Roberts says people are being "re-
enserfed". The promised land benefits only the top 1%. Globalized
poverty, unemployment, and human misery grow more institutionalized.
Monetary madness combined with austerity when stimulus is needed
assures that hard times will get harder. Irresponsible policy makers bear
full responsibility.

September 6, 2012 was Draghi day. Irrational Super Mario
exuberance made headlines. The President of the European Central
Bank explained what ECB watchers already knew. At his Frankfort press
conference, he said that Governing Council members agreed to unlimited
bond buying, called Outright Monetary Transactions (OMT).

Bundesbank President Jens Weidmann alone dissented calling
Draghi's plan "tantamount to financing governments by printing
banknotes." On August 29, 2012, Weidmann said bond purchases were
"too close to state financial via the money press for me. The central bank
cannot fundamentally solve the problems this way. It runs the risk of
creating new problems."[2]

OMT will target government bonds with one-three year
maturities. Longer-dated debt with residual maturities of that duration
will be included. Purchases ostensibly will be sterilized to keep the money
supply neutral. Don't bet on it. Earlier ECB promises fell short. Draghi
hopes to contain borrowing costs but at best he'll buy time. Since crisis
conditions emerged in fall 2007, every plan that has been tried has failed..

Draghi's plan involves conditionality. One analyst calls it
"Eurocrat-speak for debtor countries to agree to wear the particular
austerity hair shirt we have designed for them before they get any dough."
Countries needing help must request it. Spain and Italy haven't asked
for any help, as at this writing. Rome wants Madrid to go first. Spain
wants conditions waived. Since the conditions involve strict austerity,
implementing them assures greater trouble, not less.

ECB rules prohibit direct state financing. As a result, secondary
market purchases are planned. Even though the ECB's preferred creditor
status was waived, removing the requirement for central bank repayments
ahead of private ones,

Draghi's plan solves nothing. He kicked the can down the road,
leaving many questions unanswered. The ECB has been notoriously
unsuccessful in soaking up excess liquidity. Keeping inflation in check
won't be easy. Deep-seated problems are worsening. Bond-buying can't
substitute for sound policies. Markets paid no attention to Draghi's futile

effort. Short-term fixes mean higher valuations, and the eventual day of reckoning can be delayed but not denied.

The ECB's earlier Securities Market Program (SMP) failed. Citibank strategist Jamie Seale believes OMT won't fare better. He called it dangerous. Will it do anything more than buy short-term relief? It's no solution, he stressed. "The economic backdrop remains dire."[3] The SMP initially sent peripheral nations' sovereign yields lower, but this positive result didn't last long. Moreover, Draghi may intend to rely on rhetoric to do most of the heavy lifting. Unfulfilled promises only work for so long.

Goldman Sachs also dissed him. It called OMT SMP 2.0.[4] It said no easy way out of crisis conditions exists. An ECB declaration about being *pari passu* leaves unanswered questions relating to voluntary debt restructuring. It also provides no assurance about sound policy measures following promises. Why now when not earlier.

Bank of America economist Laurence Boone doubted OMT's success, saying Draghi's plan is more negative than positive. Conditionality was tougher than expected.[5] The IMF's role as monitor means Big Brother is watching. These factors lessen the likelihood that troubled countries will seek help or as much as they might have otherwise. Draghi announced no yield targets, no bond purchases ex-ante transparency, and no technical details on how OMT differs from SMP. Ireland and Portugal won't qualify for help until they regain market access. Greece is too far gone to help. Peripheral banks aren't provided relief. Other reservations were raised.

JPMorgan Asset Management's Michael Cembalest said Draghi may have to engineer a massive debt restructuring and take huge losses. In a note to clients, he explained: "Europe is conducting one of the most unorthodox experiments of the last 100 years (a competitiveness adjustment mostly through wage and price declines instead of currency devaluation), and they are making it up as they go."[6] Euro countries face problems that won't quit. Peripheral nations are deeply troubled. Massive capital outflows hammer them. Southern Europe is experiencing the greatest amount of capital flight "the modern world may have ever seen."

Cembalest's bottom line is that Draghi may be in way over his head. He's holding on to "trillions in loans and bonds that the private sector won't want to own unless there is a miraculous rebound in growth and employment." It's nowhere in sight. He dubbed the ECB the "European Creosote Bank." He can't explain what he means by that except to say it relates to a fictional character eating "several plates of mussels, pate de foie gras, beluga caviar, eggs benedict, leek tarts, frogs' legs," and other assorted delicacies washed down with bottles of expensive wines, champagne and ale. The result isn't pretty.

Other analysts call Draghi's plan short-term relief at best. It's a financial equivalent of France's Maginot line. Its vulnerability is clear. Outflanking it is likely. Instead of addressing problems responsibly, Draghi and political leaders opt for punishing austerity, rising unemployment, lower investment and consumption, deeper recession, and eventually a Eurozone breakup.

Progressive Radio News Hour regular Jack Rasmus warns regularly about trouble on air. ECB policies have had "virtually no impact" on Eurozone economies or their "drift into recession." Draghi said inter-bank lending is dysfunctional. It's not working. "When inter-bank lending shuts down," says Rasmus, "bank to non-bank business and bank to consumer lending quickly declines." Recession is further exacerbated. In 2007-08, it happened. History is now repeating. Rasmus believes the Libor scandal may be this year's subprime mortgage debacle equivalent. It may trigger the next banking crisis. How things play out remains to be seen. The immediate effect is declining confidence in banks and how they do business. "The key transmission mechanism between the banking crisis and spreading European recession is bank lending contraction: banks to other banks, banks to governments, and banks to non-bank businesses and consumer households," Rasmus says.

As lending erodes, so do economies. Forced austerity exacerbates crisis conditions. There is growing evidence of how troubled EU economies are. Throughout Europe, manufacturing has contracted. Business and consumer confidence are sinking. Investment is down. So are government revenues. Unemployment is rising. Less household income and lower consumption follow. Sovereign debt levels rise. So does instability when compounded by more austerity.

Policy makers know that everything that has been tried so far has failed. Instead of addressing the crisis conditions responsibly, they keep kicking the can down the road. They're also packaging old wine in new bottles, hoping earlier failures will magically succeed this time.

Don't bet on it.

Germany's High Court paid no attention to it when, on September 12, 2012, it capitulated to the bankers. It declared the road clear to create a 500 billion euro rescue fund by rejecting a petition to block it. Two Eurozone rescue schemes exist. One of them, the European Financial Stability Facility (EFSF) is already running out of funds so Germany's High Court approved a new European Stability Mechanism (ESM), which will function as a permanent firewall for the eurozone with a maximum lending capacity of €500 billion to cover all bailout applications from any eurozone state troubled by financial instability.Originally the ESM was scheduled to take effect July 1 but that was delayed as Germany's parliament was still debating it and Constitutional Court approval was required.

The German parliament could have linked passage to a change in its constitutional law, thereby requiring Germany's first post-war national referendum to approve it. But it stopped short of doing that and instead approved a plan that lacks legitimacy, and in the end won't work.On the one hand, countries are running out of resources. On the other, the ECB has few bullets left. Repackaged same old, same old assures failure. Constitutional approval changes nothing.

With approval of the ESM came conditions. The Financial Times[7] said those imposed appear less onerous than feared. The Court ruled Germany's maximum 190 billion euro liability can't be increased without its ESM representative approving it. According to Court President Andreas Vosskuhle: "[No] provision of this treaty may be interpreted in a way that establishes higher payment obligations for the Federal Republic of Germany without the agreement of the German representative." It also insures Bundestag involvement. Under German law accompanying ESM approval, the parliament must approve its representative's positions. It's unclear if full parliamentary or budget committee voting is required. Another condition mandates that the Bundestag and upper chamber Bundesrat (representing federal states) be kept fully informed about bailout fund activities. Vosskuhle called the Court ruling provisional. Full proceedings will follow with a final decision expected in December. The Court plans a full review of ESM's legality. At the same time, it said it won't accept ESM interpretations to permit direct ECB borrowing.

ESM and EFSF will operate in parallel until mid-2013. At that time, ESM will be on its own. Germany must provide 27% of its funds. Critics warn amounts will end up being much greater than anticipated. While ESM will have 700 billion euros in capital,only 500 billion maximum can be loaned. Troubled Spain and Italy need multiples that amount. There aren't enough resources available to provide it. A push come to shove moment awaits. It's just a matter of time. It may arrive sooner than expected, since economic conditions are dire and worsening.

Responsible observers agree: Germany's High Court acted irresponsibly. The ESM may provide short-term relief (at best) but it doesn't resolve crisis conditions. One analyst called it Super Mario's bluff. It's more feel good than real good. Troubled Spain and Italy are required to supply 30% of ESM resources. How can they in effect bail themselves out?

On September 13, 2012 the Fed announced QE 3. Pimco head Bill Gross tweeted Bernanke plans to buy mortgages "till the cows come home." QE 3 is open-ended with near zero short-term rates. Bernanke's move suggests desperation. What does he know, we don't, and why now? Things aren't as they seem. They're worse.

Troubled Eurozone countries are imploding. Obama practically begged Angela Merkel to keep things intact until post-election. Greece is bankrupt. Only its obituary remains to be written. Portugal and Ireland are sinking. So is Italy. Spain is practically coming apart. It's been deteriorating for years. In August alone, depositors withdrew 70 billion euros from Spanish banks. Their combined market cap is 114 billion euros. They need 20 billion more euros monthly to keep operating. These fund outflows cause enormous pressure. Collapse may be impossible to prevent. Nationalization hasn't helped. Bankia was taken over but its problems persist. It just needed another 5.4 billion rescue package. For sure it'll need lots more.

Spain's regions are cratering. Andalusia, Valencia, Murcia and Catalonia requested federal help without conditions. Major problems across the country look intractable. Spain asked the ECB for 100 billion euros for its banks. It needs sovereign debt help. It won't accept conditions. Its economy is too weak. It also rejects external interference in its internal affairs. It's got plenty on its hands dealing with public outrage. For example, half of all working aged youths are unemployed.

Conditions are combustible, and not just in Spain. One wrong-headed move too many could ignite things. People can take only so much pain before they explode. Germany is Europe's strongest economy but it's weakening. George Soros said it's heading for depression in six months because of wrongheaded policies. It's bearing too much of the burden for other troubled EU countries. Germany's debt to GDP ratio is 90%. It's already committed over 2.1 trillion euros in bailout help. It's spending itself to oblivion if this doesn't stop. At the same time, it's force-feeding austerity when stimulus is needed. Why?

Perhaps Bernanke's QE 3 funds are earmarked for Europe. Call it backdoor bailout help. ECB money creation is limited while Bernanke can print all he wants. It's no secret that if Europe collapses, America and the global economy will follow while China's heading for a hard landing. This coordinated central bank intervention on top of everything done so far suggests panic. Things are worse than they seem. Bernanke, Draghi, and BoE's Mervyn King are scared stiff. Their policy appears to be do something, anything (other than ease austerity), no matter how long the odds. Again, why?

Few expected an open-ended Fed pledge to buy $40 billion worth of mortgage bonds monthly and continue Operation Twist. Officially it's called the Maturity Extension Program. It exchanges short-term debt for longer maturities. In theory, it's to lower interest rates on 10-year Treasuries. It also represents QE without printing more money and thereby dampens inflationary pressures.

But for how long will it do so in an environment of money madness? Official numbers mask the high level of inflation. Based on its

1980s model, Shadowstats estimates that the inflation rate is around 9%. Everyone who eats, drives a car, heats and/or air conditions a home, has health insurance and other medical expenses, and/or pays tuition bills knows inflation is high and rising. Household budgets are sorely stressed.

Lloyds TSB Bank analyst said Bernanke was true to his "Helicopter Ben" reputation. Pimco's Mohamed headlined his Financial Times op-ed "QE 3 is a sign of the Fed's policy purgatory," saying:

> [T]he Federal Reserve confirmed on Thursday that it is operating in policy purgatory: incapable of delivering the good economic outcomes it desires, yet unable to exit from an experimental policy stance that risks a widening array of collateral damage and unintended consequences.[8]

Previous actions have failed. Economic conditions may be worse than most think. On August 31, Bernanke cited "daunting economic challenges." He expressed "grave concern" about high unemployment. He knows headline U 3 deception masks its severity. Youth unemployment is dangerously high. Workers leaving the labor force in huge numbers shows how bad things are.

Monetary policy is the only game in town. Political Washington force feeds austerity with much more of it coming. Conditions aren't uncertain—they're awful and heading south. The Fed policy suggests panic mode. Will anything it does help?

> History and detailed analyses of the problems underpinning America's prolonged economic malaise suggest these well-intentioned measures will again fail to secure a much better economic situation....
>
> This is also behind the widening gap between economists urging the Fed to do even more and those favoring less."

At the same time, Bernanke said "monetary policy cannot by itself (deliver) what a broader and more balanced set of economic policies might achieve" Despite that clear admission, any such policies are absent. Fed bullets haven't worked so far. Increasingly they're delivering less bang for the buck. They're treading water, buying time, and as far as the eye can see, they're doing so "in policy purgatory" until the whole house of cards (that Greenspan and Bernanke built) collapses. They've only got themselves to blame.

A Wall Street Journal op-ed piece headlined "Bernanke Unbound,"[9] noted thatBernanke entered a "brave new world of unlimited monetary easing." He offered markets a bottomless punchbowl. His actions contradict his caveat that monetary policy "is no panacea." It can't save the economy by itself.

Some ask: "When does the Fed take some responsibility for policies that fail in their self-professed goal of spurring growth, rather than blaming everyone else while claiming to be the only policy hero?" What about shortchanged savers? Bernanke's hope for long-term relief doesn't soothe. Keynes said by then we're dead. Bernanke isn't superman. He's a super con-manpushing on a string. He already caused high inflation. Consumers see it daily. How much higher is tolerable? Why aren't these and other core issues factored into decision-making? "The deeper into exotic monetary easing the Fed goes, the harder it will also be to unwind in a timely fashion."

Bernanke says: don't worry. That's what central bankers always say. Fulfillment doesn't match promises. Boosting equity prices short-term helps Obama. "For all the back-slapping" and pontificating for nearly five years, bottom line Fed analysis acknowledges things are rotten, "job creation stinks," and the policies that have been tried have failed. At the same time, his move highlights the law of unintended consequences. He likely made things worse, not better. He weakened the dollar, strengthened the euro, added another EU headwind, boosted commodity prices, made things less affordable, created more instability, and won't deliver what some observers hope. One analyst said "let 'em eat stocks and housing" doesn't work. His policy doesn't spell relief. It's more feel good than do good. Super-low rates haven't helped. Economic numbers across the board are weak and heading south.

But QE 3 isn't about more liquidity. There's more than enough around. Thirty year mortgage rates hover around 3.5%. Banks are hoarding cash, sitting on over $1.5 trillion in reserves. Corporations have around $2 trillion. Interest rates can't go much lower. At issue are economic risk and inflation. Monetary policy alone can't help. The more freely it's applied, the less effective it gets, and if there is too much liquidity, soaring prices defeat it.

At the same time, what some have called the "fiscal cliff" looms next year, possibly pitching the economy into a new recession because of substantial tax rises and government spending cuts due to hit early next year unless Congress agrees to cancel or delay them. So are three straight negative Institute for Supply Management (ISM)[10] reads, revealing dangerously high unemployment, and overall economic conditions heading south.

Coordinated central bank intervention is in play. It includes Bank of England's unconventional "funding for lending." The ECB promised open-ended sovereign debt buying up to three years duration provided governments request it and accept stiff austerity conditions. Now there's QE 3. Expect the Bank of Japan to have its say.

Together with Operation Twist, the Fed plans buying $85 billion through yearend and open-ended QE thereafter. If it buys mortgage backed securities long enough, it may end up owning them all, and then what? "Anything goes" is policy. The Fed said it will "undertake additional asset purchases and employ other tools as appropriate until such improvement is achieved in the context of price stability." Call the latter alone a giant X factor. Since the Fed's most radical ever policies for over four years haven't worked, expect no change this time.

Economic growth is fundamental. A multi-decade long Japanese malaise or something much worse looks likely. Median family income declined two straight years. In 2011, it was 8.1% lower than 2007. Household net worth dropped for an unprecedented five straight years with no end in sight to its free fall. Housing remains weak and troubled. Manufacturing is dropping.

Global weakening is apparent. US July European exports fell 6.6%. China's August EU exports plunged 13% year-over-year. Japan heads for negative GDP growth. Weekly US jobless claims hit a two month high. Capex plans are down 3.7% next year. So are hiring plans. The latest JOLTS data (Job Openings and Labor Turnover Survey) shows weakness. The year-over-year trend is down. New hires are depressed. Most other economic numbers are soft.

Revenue and profit declines are increasing. What's happening in America and across Europe is hitting everywhere. Everything's coming up weeds, not roses. Poverty is high and rising. So is public anger. At the same time, sequestered budget cuts are coming next year. It's madness when stimulus is needed. They're automatic under the 2011 Budget Control Act (BCA). Initial ones total $1.2 trillion. Much more will follow over the next decade. Social benefits will be hit hard. They take effect on January 1, 2013. Sequestered means mandatory across-the-board cuts. Congress and Obama agreed. Legislators have little discretion. Allegedly all programs will be affected. Don't bet on it. Defense is sacrosanct. So is corporate favoritism. Households needing help will be hurt most. It's been that way for years. Expect worse ahead.

Cuts are intended for deficit reduction but nonetheless the deficit is rising exponentially. It'll keep doing so as far as the eye can see. Claims that the deficit is doing otherwise simply provides a cover to slash Medicare, Medicaid, and other vital social services.

At the same time, nothing slows America's war machine nor will corporate favorites be denied. The bipartisan complicity of the Republican and Democratic Parties assures it. Pain is the name of the game for most people. Occupy Wall Street is right. The only solution is world revolution. Europe shows some signs of approaching that threshold, but not a hint of it is in sight in America. Yet.

ENDNOTES

1   <http://www.globalresearch.ca/the-revolution-from-above-the-wipeout-of-americans-hopes/>

2   <http://www.spiegel.de/international/europe/spiegel-interview-with-bundesbank-president-jens-weidmann-a-852285.html>

3   <http://www.businessinsider.com/citi-ecb-new-plan-omt-smp-2012-9>

4   <http://www.businessinsider.com/goldman-has-the-most-devastating-description-of-the-ecbs-new-bond-buying-scheme-2012-9>

5   <http://www.businessinsider.com/bofa-ecb-not-about-to-buy-bonds-2012-9>

6   <http://www.businessinsider.com/jpmorgan-ecb-engineer-a-debt-renegotation-2012-9>

7   <http://www.ft.com/intl/cms/s/23f69368-fcaf-11e1-9dd2-00144feabdc0,Authorised=false.html?_i_location=http%3A%2F%2Fwww.ft.com%2Fcms%2Fs%2F0%2F23f69368-fcaf-11e1-9dd2-00144feabdc0.html&_i_referer=#axzz291HyHAT9>

8   <http://blogs.ft.com/the-a-list/2012/09/13/qe3-is-a-sign-of-the-feds-policy-purgatory/?Authorised=false#axzz28k2gMyPO>

9   <http://online.wsj.com/article/SB10000872396390444709004577649831698298106.html?mod=googlenews_wsj>

10   <http://www.ism.ws/ismreport/nonmfgrob.cfm>

13

US CITIES GOING BANKRUPT

In past decades, many US municipalities have declared bankruptcy. Since 1981, 42 cases were filed. Ten came in the past four years. Given hard times getting harder, what's happening now is unprecedented since the Great Depression. Cities occasionally declare bankruptcy, but in America, it's happening more often. There are other cities in dire financial straits which soon may follow.

San Bernardino, CA is the latest. On July 11, The New York Times headlined "Third City In California Votes to Seek Bankruptcy," sayingthat officials have no choice. They can't meet payroll obligations through summer. "Faced with a budget shortfall of $45 million and city coffers that have already been drained, the San Bernardino City Council voted on Tuesday to file for bankruptcy." Interim city manager Andrea Travis-Miller said:"I am concerned about our ability to make payroll, not only in the next 30 days but also in the next 60 to 90 days. A major restructuring of this organization is needed."

California cities have two Chapter 9 bankruptcy options. They can either hire a third-party mediator to negotiate with unions and creditors or declare a fiscal emergency.

San Bernardino chose the latter way. Depression conditions ravage the city. Many others face similar problems. Stockton and Mammoth Lakes declared bankruptcy earlier. Other financially strapped cities and towns around the state and country may follow.

It's hard keeping up with many troubled municipalities, counties, school systems, and other public services potentially facing bankruptcy.

In December 2010, financial analyst Meredith Whitney told 60 Minutes[1] that over 100 US cities could go bust in the next year. "There's not a doubt on my mind that you will see a spate of municipal bond defaults. You can see fifty to a hundred sizeable defaults—more. This will amount to hundreds of billions of dollars' worth of defaults," she said.

States' spending exceeds revenues by hundreds of billions of dollars. Pension funds are $1 trillion in the red. Things are worse now than in 2010. While Meredith's prediction hasn't unfolded as fast as she feared, she may be proved right and then some before the crisis conditions subside.

Paul Craig Roberts, former Assistant Treasury Secretary under Reagan, sees America's economy collapsing. He wrote about it[2] and told Progressive Radio News Hour listeners. that he wonders if it'll happen before Washington clashes with Russia and China militarily. He suggests an ominous doomsday choice—going down either financially or in a mushroom shaped cloud.

Americans have achieved nothing from their wars but debt which can't be repaid. As Michael Hudson says, debts that can't be paid, won't be. Hudson calls it a "common denominator throughout recorded history."

Adam Smith said governments never repay debts. When they become too burdensome, defaults follow. The possibility that US cities and municipalities may fall like tenpins looms.

Since 2008, budgets have been severely slashed. But slashing budgets becomes counterproductive because austerity assures disaster. With fewer people employed at lower pay, revenues can't match expenses.

Higher taxes make things worse. People can't buy goods and services without jobs and decent incomes.

Instead of going for broke by stimulating growth, America, like European countries, are simply going broke. Bad policies beget bad results. Sacrificing economies and households to enrich bankers assures failure. In America it's happening one foreclosure, lost job, bankrupt city and municipality at a time. Instead of government fixing problems, it's leaving them to fester.

Until the 1930s, it was legally impossible for US cities to declare bankruptcy. Municipal legislation permitting it didn't exist. The 1934 Bankruptcy Act changed things. Cities and municipalities were included. These earlier rules became today's US Bankruptcy Code Chapter 9, available exclusively to cities and towns. But municipal bankruptcies don't extinguish debt. Reorganization follows.

Cities can break untenable contracts and get more attractive financing. In 1994, Orange County, California, home to some of the country's most affluent communities, went bust due to bad speculative investments. It's. In May 2008, Vallejo, California declared bankruptcy. Last-ditch rescue efforts to prevent it failed. Up to that point, a California city that large had never taken this route. At the time, city manager Joseph Tanner said:"This has been a long frustrating process for everyone. There are no winners here tonight." Vallejo's city council voted unanimously to approve Chapter 9 bankruptcy protection. Its finances were in shambles.

Across America, cities and towns face the same dilemma. It's not pretty when mayors and municipal managers can't meet payrolls or pay other expenses. Short of turning out the lights and shutting down municipal government, they reorganize. Life goes on as usual but not easily for many. Ordinary people suffer the most. Basic services get scrubbed to the bone.

In October 2011, Jefferson County, Alabama declared Chapter 9 bankruptcy. Alabama is home to the state's most populous city, Birmingham. Its debt exceeded $4 billion. It was America's largest municipal filing in history.

Fears spread then and now about who's next. Along with many small towns, transportation and school systems, Pennsylvania's capital Harrisburg filed last year.

In late June 2012, Stockton, California declared bankruptcy. It signaled more attacks on public workers, pensions and public services throughout the country. Stockton acted after talks with bondholders and unions failed. The city released a statement saying, "(t)he city is fiscally insolvent and must seek Chapter 9" protection. This key agricultural center is now the largest US city to file. Mayor Ann Johnston said she saw "no other solution."Health care for current and retired city workers was slashed, just as it had been in Vallejo and other cities and towns. The people least able to manage suffer the most.Bankruptcy attorney Dale Ginter said labor and health insurance costs hurt municipalities—so cutting what impacts them most gets prioritized.

Stockton, Harrisburg, San Bernardino, Vallejo, and other municipal bankruptcies reflect years of Wall Street fleecing America. Crooked bankers have transformed America into an unprecedented money making racket—for bankers.

With the complicity of federal, state and local governments, they make it the old fashioned way. They steal it. Not only ordinary Americans get scammed—so do large and small municipalities.

When the other choices run out, bankruptcy's the final option. Class struggle follows, as private wealth and working households vie. A handful of winners emergewhile ordinary people lose jobs, homes, and vital services. Cherished entitlements are slashed or ended. The American dream is just a memory as super-rich elites cash in big to make more. Concentrated wealth and power never had it so good.

Detroit hasn't gone bust but it's dying. Half or more of its working aged residents have no jobs. Those with them have low-pay part-time or temp jobs.For over a century, Detroit was America's industrial heartland. It drew workers from around the country for high-paying jobs with good benefits. Now they're gone and over the last decade, half the population has left with them.Factories and neighborhoods are empty. Detroit is now America's poorest big city. Poverty, unemployment, hunger and homelessness are endemic. Former middle class residents suffer like the others. Their status reflects a national nightmare.

In October 2009, Prichard, Alabama declared bankruptcy for the second time. Mayor Ron Davis just finished paying creditors from its 1999 filing. He released a statement saying other options weren't viable.

In August 2011, Central Falls, RI declared bankruptcy. Located north of Providence, it's the state's poorest municipality. In 2010, it entered receivership. Major concessions were made. In February 2010, Central Falls High School fired all 74 teachers and 19 staff. It was part of a "turnaround plan" that never materialized. Deep concessions accompanied rehiring. Greater ones followed bankruptcy.

In March 2011, Boise County, Idaho filed for protection. It did so to buy time to figure out how to pay creditors.

Large and smaller US cities are troubled but still just short of bankruptcy. They include New York, San Diego, San Jose, San Francisco, Los Angeles, and Bell, California; Newark, Camden, Paterson, Harrison and Salem, New Jersey; Gary, Indiana; Redding, Pennsylvania; Joliet and Riverdale, Illinois; Detroit, Pontiac and Hamtramck, Michigan; Cincinnati, Honolulu, Washington; and others.

Not just cities but counties, school systems, and other municipal services face going broke since states are budget strapped. Conditions aren't getting easier. Debts that can't be paid, won't be.

As long as business as usual prioritizes bankers over economies and households, a collapse sometime in the future looks more likely than recovery. Today's grim reality portends it.

ENDNOTES

1   <http://articles.businessinsider.com/2010-12-20/markets/30034131_1_delay-payments-watch-big-test>

2   <http://www.globalresearch.ca/the-collapsing-us-economy-and-the-end-of-the-world/>

14

AMERICA'S GREAT DIVIDE BETWEEN RICH AND POOR

In 1962, Michael Harrington's *The Other America* exposed the nation's dark side, saying:

> In morality and in justice, every citizen should be committed to abolishing the other America, for it is intolerable that the richest nation in human history should allow such needless suffering.
>
> But more than that, if we solve the problem of the other America we will have learned how to solve the problems of all of America.[1]

Jack Kennedy was concerned enough to ask Walter Heller, his Council of Economic Advisor chairman, to examine the problem. In his January 8, 1964 State of the Union address, poverty levels also moved Lyndon Johnson to say that his administration "today, here and now, declares unconditional war on poverty in America." In fact, he barely scratched it. But at least he did get Congress to enact measures helping America's poor.

Inequality then was severe but today, it's unprecedented and growing. Census data show around half of US households are impoverished or bordering on it while wealthy elites are richer than ever.

In fact, government data consistently over-estimate good news and understate the bad. As a result, unprecedented numbers of US households are impoverished under protracted Main Street Depression conditions while the government and media refuse to label their situation what it is.

Contrary to government action under Kennedy and Johnson, political Washington's austerity measures actually cause greater harm.

Their shocking bipartisan indifference to human need and suffering is criminal.

The world's richest ever country boasts a poverty rate that is the highest among the industrialized nations. Homelessness and hunger levels are unprecedented. Over 20% of US families haven't enough money to buy food and need help. Over half of US children need food stamps to eat. Tens of millions have no health insurance. Those with it pay double the cost of health care in other developed nations. The policies enacted under Obama assure even tougher times ahead.

Unemployment approaches record highs. Manipulated government data hide it. Those employed work longer for less. Home foreclosures and bankruptcies affect millions. Adjusted for inflation, US median income is no higher than it was in the 1970s.

In their book titled, *Winner-Take-All Politics: How Washington Made the Rich Richer*,[2] Paul Pierson and Jacob Hacker explained how unprecedented wealth transfers to America's rich destroyed its middle class households, deepening poverty and creating a permanent underclass.

In September 2011, *Forbes* magazine's annual report on America's richest 400 showed their net worth soaring to over $1.5 trillion, up 12% from 2010.

Studies Show Shocking US Inequality

In November 2011, *The New York Times* headlined, "Middle-Class Areas Shrink as Income Gap Grows, New Report Shows,"[3] pointing to a Stanford University study titled, "Growth in the Residential Segregation of Families by Income, 1970-2009," which provided yet more proof that households living in middle income areas have declined sharply since 1970. Rising income inequality propelled those who were once better off into low-income or poverty.

Conditions now are much worse. Study author Sean Reardon said these income shifts have far-reaching implications for future generations if the present trends continue. Children are especially disadvantaged, left without access to good schools, preschool, child care, and support networks. Formerly solid middle class areas are now low-income or poor.

Income differences have profound effects. One example shows up in standardized test scores. There, the differential between rich and poor children is 40% greater than in 1970. Moreover, the gap between rich and poor college completion (a key predictor of future success) is 50% greater than it was in the 1990s. Over half the children from higher income families finish college compared to less than 10% of those from lower income households.

According to Harvard sociologist William Julius Wilson, "Rising inequality" produces a "two-tiered society ... in which the more affluent citizens live lives fundamentally different from middle and lower-income groups. This divide decreases a sense of community."

In October 2011, the Congressional Budget Office (CBO) published after-tax income data from 1979-2007, saying it grew:

- 275% for the top 1%;

- 65% for the next 19%;

- less than 40% for next 60%; and

- just 18% for the bottom 20%.

Data were adjusted for household size differentials. However, inflation adjusted measures weren't provided. These reveal far greater differences between rich and poor. According to Professor Paul Buchheit, America's top 1% tripled their after-tax income from 1980-2006, while the bottom 90% saw theirs drop over 20%. "[O]ur economy," he said, "allows a tiny percentage of us to take an inordinate amount of money from society, at an increasing rate."[4]

According to economists Emmanuel Saez and Thomas Piketty, America's income inequality was the highest in recorded history in 2007 before the current crisis began, and Census data way understate it.[5]

One Dollar for Life/economics public school teacher Robert Freeman said "[b]etween 2002 and 2006, [an] astounding three-quarters of the economy's growth was captured by the top 1%."[6] In his January 2010 Common Dreams article, he said it had "70% of all financial assets," a record high. Moreover, the bottom 40% own nothing and have a combined zero net worth!

In December 2011, the Congressional Research Service (CRS)[7] reported on income differentials from 1996-2006, saying, inflation adjusted, the gap grew by 25%. However, averages obscure variations. America's poorest 20% saw their income levels fall 6%, and if measured since 1979, the decline would have been much greater. In contrast, the top 1% earners saw incomes double from 1996-2006. Middle income earners experienced a 10% increase. In addition, income inequality as measured by the Gini coefficient increased 9% before taxes and 11% after-tax which favor income from capital gains and dividends, benefiting richer Americans most. Overall, taxes in 2006 were less progressive than in 1996. Today, the extremes are greater.

A 2011 Michael Norton/Dan Ariely study titled, "Building a Better America-One Wealth Quintile at a Time,"[8] showed the extent to which most Americans vastly underestimate today's wealth disparities. Americans believe the richest 20% control about 59% of the nation's wealth when in actuality they control about 84%, say the study authors. It fact, it's over 90%, perhaps well over.

A January 2012 Indiana University/School of Public and Environmental Affairs study titled, "At Risk: America's Poor During and After the Great Recession"[9] discussed enormous growing problems facing the nation's least advantaged. Protracted economic weakness "inflicted long-lasting damage to individuals, families, and communities," it said. It created a "near poor" and "new poor" underclass.

Long-term unemployment contributes greatly. Over four million Americans say they've been out of work over a year, the largest number since data collection began in 1948.

Young people and minorities between 18 and 34 have been hardest hit. Safety net protections are inadequate and eroding.

A Final Comment

Wrongheaded policies assure growing misery while America's rich never had it so good. That's the dilemma voters face in an election year when neither party offers solutions. Instead, they assure growing wealth disparity, greater poverty, and human misery.

Only grassroots activism can change things. OWS protests showed promise, but nothing will happen easily or quickly. The mother of all social justice struggles is just beginning. It will grow because the mounting inequalities and human needs are too intolerable to accept.

Organized people power works. Using it can beat organized money. If that's not incentive enough, what is?

ENDNOTES

1   Michael Harrington, *The Other America*, Scribner's, 1997.

2   Paul Pierson and Jacob S. Hacker, *Winner-Take-All Politics: How Washington Made the Rich Richer, and Turned Its Back on the Middle Class*, Simon & Schuster, 2010.

3   <http://www.nytimes.com/2011/11/16/us/middle-class-areas-shrink-as-income-gap-grows-report-finds.html?_r=3&>

4   < http://www.alternet.org/story/145705/the_richest_1_have_captured_america%27s_wealth_--_what%27s_it_going_to_take_to_get_it_back>

5   < http://www.businessinsider.com/us-income-inequality-is-frightening-and-much-worse-than-we-thought-2009-9>

6   < http://www.commondreams.org/view/2010/01/17>

7   < http://taxprof.typepad.com/taxprof_blog/2011/12/crs-on.html>

8   < http://www.people.hbs.edu/mnorton/norton%20ariely.pdf>
9   <http://www.tavistalks.com/remakingamerica/wp-content/
uploads/2011/12/Indiana-University_White-Paper_EMBARGOED-
UNTIL-WED__JAN.-11-AT-8AM1.pdf>

15

HARD RIGHT EXTREMISM IN AMERICA AND EUROPE

Anders Breivik's July 22, 2011 Oslo rampage, killing 77 people, 69 of them teenagers, highlighted a problem far greater than the actions of a single socio-path. The implications for Europe and elsewhere are huge.

In 1932, Mussolini declared the 20th century a "Fascist century," saying: "It is to be expected that this century may be that of authority, a century of the 'Right,' a Fascist century." He claimed it would "sav[e] Western civilization." For what, he didn't explain.

Post-WW I, Fascism's roots emerged. At the time, Western civilization was thought to be decadent, destructive, and in decline. In his essay titled, "Fascism: Doctrine and Institutions," Mussolini said, "Fascism denies, in democracy, the absurd conventional untruth of political equality dressed out in the garb of collective responsibility." He called it the "complete opposite" of Marxist belief in class struggle as the driving force for social progress and justice. He said "[f]ascism should more appropriately be called Corporatism because it is a merger of State and corporate power."

That definition applies today. Corporatism's alliance with political Washington reflects Mussolini's ideology. It's been building for decades. In America, hardline anti-government groups like the Sovereign Citizen movement highlight how far right America has shifted since the 1980s. Their adherents (Sovereigns) believe they alone should decide what laws to obey or ignore, not elected officials, judges, juries or law enforcement bodies. They also oppose paying taxes, promote racial hatred, attract white supremacists, and resort to violence to assert their will. In addition, they subscribe to other extremist views, advocating a subculture run exclusively by their rules. Without central leadership, it's impossible to know the size of this movement, though it's believed to be in the thousands.

America's Militia movement is also politically significant. They're paramilitaries against government restricting their rights, especially to bear arms. It's an outgrowth of independent survivalist, anti-tax, and other right-wing Patriot movement subculture groups, who believe government is hostile to their freedom.

More recently, America's Tea Party phenomenon reflects political Washington's sharp right turn. Stressing fiscal responsibility, constitutionally limited government and free market fundamentalism, demagogic extremists aroused millions of working Americans to support policies that were against their own interests. Clever mind manipulation convinced these dupes they're doing the right thing, no matter how self-destructive.

Funded by extremist right-wing groups, as well as billionaires like David and Charles Koch, the movement gained national recognition in media-hyped mid-2009 congressional town hall protests against Obamacare, banker and other bailouts, fiscal excesses, and bogus claims about Obama's social agenda. (Obama in fact is a rock-hard conservative and doesn't have one.)

In February 2010, the Tea Party's Nashville, Tennessee national convention increased its prominence. It highlighted shifting America further right on the pretext of popular opposition to big government and fiscal irresponsibility. As a result, hard line extremists attracted mostly middle income Americans who were facing lost jobs, foreclosed homes, and economic uncertainty. They should have shifted left, not right, creating a groundswell for addressing popular needs instead of blaming big government.

But they didn't. Demagogues took advantage of their malaise and aroused millions, aided by daily Fox News support and its lunatic fringe hosts such as Glenn Beck (now gone), Bill O'Reilly, and others, who rage against big government, hyping an extremist agenda. Maliciously, they spread fear to attract growing numbers of adherents, largely mindless that their best interests are being compromised rather than addressed.

The manipulation of the major media is essential, whether against big government, alleged terrorists, or anything left of right-wing politics, and it's easily able to morph into something more sinister.

In his 2003 article titled, "Fascism Anyone?" political scientist Laurence W. Britt discussed its 14 common elements, saying: "These basic characteristics are more prevalent and intense in some regimes than in others, but they all share some level of similarity."[1]

Let us elaborate on these, below.

(1) "Powerful and continuing nationalism." This includes display

flags, lapel pins, and other patriotic nationalist expressions, rallying people for a common cause.

(2) "Disdain for the importance of human rights" and civil liberties, in the belief that these hinder ruling elitist power and their ability to get things done.

(3) "Identification of enemies/scapegoats as a unifying cause," shifting blame for their own and society's perceived failures, "channel[ling] frustration in controlled directions" not harmful to powerful interests, and vilifying targeted groups for political advantage.

(4) "The supremacy of the military" and avid militarism, allocating a disproportionate share of national wealth and resources for the military, and adopting a reverential attitude towards it and uniformed personnel.

(5) "Rampant sexism," viewing women as second-class citizens.

(6) "Controlled mass media," whether in public or private hands, so long as it promotes power elite policies.

(7) "Obsession with national security," using it as an instrument of internal and external belligerence and oppression.

(8) "Religion and government are intertwined," with militant self-appointed defenders of the nation's dominant religion at the expense of one or more others, deemed inferior or threatening.

(9) "Corporate power is protected," and deployed to generate economic power, military production, and social control.

(10) "Labor power is suppressed " leaving political and corporate dominance unchallenged.

(11) "Disdain for intellectuals and the arts," because they represent intellectual and academic freedom, which is viewed as subversive to national security and political control.

(12) "Obsession with crime and punishment," handling them by draconian criminal justice measures and practices.

(13) "Rampant cronyism and corruption," whereby power elites

enrich themselves at the expense of others less fortunate.

(14) "Fraudulent elections," manipulated for desired results by disenfranchising opposition voters or simply rigging the process.

These characteristics describe America today. It's democratic in name only. It's run by powerful elitists for their own interests at the expense of all others.

Huey Long once said fascism will arrive "wrapped in an American flag." In his book "Friendly Fascism,"[2] Hunter College Professor Bertram Gross called Ronald Reagan its prototype ruler. Gross distinguished 1980s America from classic models in Germany, Italy and Japan,describing a slow, powerful "drift toward greater concentration of power and wealth in a repressive Big Business-Big Government," a Big Brother alliance that leads "toward a new and subtly manipulative form of corporatist serfdom." Its friendly face conceals hard line policies revealing Machiavellian techniques to exploit others to achieve and maintain wealth and power.

In 2010, Noam Chomsky said: "I'm just old enough to have heard a number of Hitler's speeches on the radio, and I have a memory of the texture and the tone of the cheering mobs, and I have the dread sense of the dark clouds of fascism gathering" here at home.

At the time, Weimar Germany "was the peak of Western civilization and was regarded as a model of democracy." How quickly things changed.

In 1928, Nazis got 2% of the vote. By 1930, millions supported them during growing hard times. Moreover, people were tired of government favoring powerful interests and ignoring popular grievances. They lurched to the right seeking something better. They succumbed to appeals about "the greatness of the nation, defending it against threats, and carrying out the will of eternal providence." When workers, farmers, petit bourgeoisie, and Christian groups supported it, "the center very quickly collapsed."

Echoes of that time "reverberat(e)" today, Chomsky stressed. "These are lessons to keep in mind," especially after Congress abolished due process rights, letting military authorities indefinitely detain US citizens without charges, trial, or evidence. By doing that, they institutionalized tyranny. Henceforth, challenging state power endangers anyone doing it.

Today's Duopoly-Run America

On issues mattering most, little distinguishes Republicans from

Democrats. Supporting militarism, permanent wars, corporate dominance, and police state harshness, they both represent wealth and power interests at the expense of public needs and rights.

As a result, more than ever, a bogus American democracy is ushering in a police state apparatus that sacrifices human rights and civil liberties in order to protect national security, wealth, power, and control. Examples include:

(1) An array of pre and post-9/11 anti-terrorist measures.

(2) Decades of illegal surveillance of individuals and activist groups, now more virulent and sophisticated than ever under Obama. Notably, these include unchecked surveillance powers, including warrantless wiretapping, accessing personal records, monitoring financial transactions, and tracking emails, Internet and cell phone use to gather secret evidence for prosecutions. As a result, more than ever under Obama's leadership, America has become a repressive Big Brother society, targeting anyone challenging its lawless rule.

(3) A war on free expression, dissent, and constitutional freedoms, using the courts to enforce repression, especially since the 1996 Antiterrorism and Effective Penalty Act. This Act eased surveillance restrictions, included draconian death penalty and habeas-stripping provisions, and smoothed the way for the 2001 Patriot Act and the repressive measures that followed.

Alone, in fact, the *Patriot Act* erodes four Bill of Rights freedoms, including:

- Fifth and Fourteenth Amendments due process rights by permitting indefinite detentions;

- First Amendment freedom of association; and

- Fourth Amendment right to be free from unreasonable searches and seizures, and more.

In November 2002, the Bush administration's Homeland Security Act (HSA) combined formerly separate government agencies into a more sweeping authoritarian apparatus. Thereafter, it's been used repressively. Obama uses it like Bush. He usurped unprecedented power for total control, sacrificing freedoms for national security. As a result, America enforces police state harshness. Merriam-Webster defines a police state as:

> a political unit characterized by repressive governmental control of political, economic, and social life usually by an arbitrary exercise of power by police and especially secret police in place of regular operation of administration and judicial organs of the government according to publicly known legal procedures. America has in place constitutional/statute laws, as well as administrative and legal procedures, yet the government skirts them willfully to assert control.

It's a short leap to tyrannical rule. Whether or not it has been announced, the government's iron fist asserts fascist power.

The Right Turn in Europe

Anders Breivik's rampage signifies something far more sinister than just his mass shooting in Norway of innocent teenagers. It's symptomatic of a growing European ideological extremism, transcending a single atrocity.

Xenophobia is one of its manifestations. Merriam-Webster defines it as "fear[(ing\ and hat[ing] strangers or foreigners or anything strange or foreign." During hard times, large numbers of people are affected, though few commit violence.

The Tea Party protests reflect this phenomenon in America. They support policies that are far to the right of center. They rail against big government. They're mindless about flourishing state socialism, yet want America and its ill-defined honor restored.

Throughout Europe, in nearly all countries, there are parties wanting foreigners evicted so that the countries can be run by "rightful citizens". It's little taken into account how many of those "rightful citizens" have ancestral roots elsewhere.

Moreover, fascist parties notably once had leftist leaders who then turned to the right. Mussolini, in fact, invented the word "fascism" and practiced it destructively with his Axis partners. Today's model is more subtle, but just as dangerous. It erodes democracy and social justice to be able to exercise unchallenged power.

As a result, socially democratic rule is disappearing. Neoliberalism replaced it, notably in Nordic countries, which are run by right-wing parties . Except for Norway, which is governed by a Labour/

Socialist Left/Centre Party coalition, its so-called red-green alternative.

Challenging it is Norway's Progress Party: conservative, xenophobic, and hard-line. Perhaps Breivik's rampage warned Labour to shift right, tone down its criticism of Israel, think twice about supporting an independent Palestine, and remain committed to NATO's global imperium.

Sweden's right turn had observers asking about European social democracy's future. Is it quiescent or lost? Last September, Sweden's Social Democrats lost badly, their worst showing since 1914The right-wing Alliance prevailed. A far right anti-immigrant party won seats for the first time. This matters because Sweden's virtuous middle straddled capitalist and communist extremes and now, for the first time in over 80 years, it's over. Sweden no longer represents social democratic values. If these values can be lost in Sweden, Norway, and other Nordic countries, can they exist anywhere? Is an era of global tyranny fast approaching?

Notably since the 1990s, Social Democrats systematically undermined their own former policies, losing popular support as a result. After its electoral loss, *Svenska Dagbladet* (a daily newspaper) said Sweden's political landscape changed dramatically under "a center-right government without a majority, a crashed social democracy, and a kingmaker party with roots in the far right."

There's rising ethno-nationalist/anti-multiculturalism throughout Europe in addition to in Denmark and Norway. Is fascism a short leap ahead? Nazism arose from hard times. It demanded change that included radical right turns, intolerance, totalitarianism, and global wars, creating upheaval and societies that were unfit to live in.

Fascism threatens Europe, America, and everywhere that the kind of conditions exist that tend to transform liberal democracies to tyranny. It destroyed Weimar Germany and shifted Great Society America to right-wing/hard line rule. After abolishing due process rights for US citizens, the US government is headed toward full-blown tyranny.

Famed journalist George Seldes (1890-1995) saw fascism flourish in the 1930s. He worried it could derail New Deal America. In his 1934 book titled*Iron, Blood and Profits*, he discussed a "world-wide munitions racket," citing WW I militarists and weapons makers in Europe and America. "Merchants of death" he called them, promoting "imperialism [and] colonization—by means of war... the healthfulness of their business depend[ing] on slaughter. The more wars," the greater their riches.

Seldes' 1943 book titled *Facts and Fascism* returned to the theme, explaining "Fascism on the Home Front" in Part One, called "The Big Money and Big Profits in Fascism." In Parts Two and Three, he discussed "Native Fascist Forces" in industry and the media of his day. A shadow of today's in influence and reach, that media cheerled wars, corporate extremism, and repressive laws. It's a short leap from this kind of broadcasting to full-blown tyranny, and it threatens America more today than it did then.

In his 1935 novel titled, *It Can't Happen Here*, Sinclair Lewis also saw fascism coming in hard times, led by a charismatic, self-styled reformer/populist champion—a con man exploiting human misery. He recounted Merzelium "Buzz" Windrip's rise to power and how his promise to restore prosperity equitably hid his alliance with corporatist interests and religious ideologues. Windrip capitalized on hard times to establish militarism and unconstitutional governance. He convened military tribunals for civilians and called dissenters traitors. He institutionalized tyranny, put political enemies in concentration camps, and created Minute Men paramilitaries to terrorize anyone opposing him.He destroyed democracy, declared martial law, usurped dictatorial powers, circumvented Congress, and made himself supreme ruler.

If it could happen during Roosevelt's New Deal era, as Lewis said, indeed it can happen now. If then, why not now—when con men like Bush and Obama exploit conditions to enact police state laws, crack down on dissent, wage imperial wars, homeland ones on scapegoats, and serve powerful interests at the expense of others.

September 11 accelerated American extremism. Breivik's rampage notched it up in Europe. The fascist seeds he planted there took hold. Maybe now they'll grow and flourish. That prospect should arouse popular resistance against what no one should tolerate anywhere.

ENDNOTES

1   < http://globalresearch.ca/articles/BRI411A.html>
2   Bertram Gross, ***Friendly Fascism*** *The New Face of Power in America*, South End Press, 1980.

16

CONSTITUTIONALLY PROTECTED SYMBOLIC SPEECH

If there's anything America bills itself as upholding, it's free speech. A significant dimension of this is the right of symbolic speech, which includes leafleting, picketing, demonstrating, marching, speaking publicly, flag burning, displaying t-shirts, armbands, banners and placards, sit-ins, as well as camping out in public places.

With some exceptions, all of the above have First Amendment protection. Numerous Supreme Court decisions addressed the issue. Some agreed. Others didn't. For example, in *Hague v. Committee for Industrial Organization* (1939), Justice Owen Roberts expressed the Court's plurality opinion, saying:

> Wherever the title of streets and parks may rest, they have immemorially been held in trust for the use of the public and, time out of mind, have been used for purposes of assembly, communicating thoughts between citizens, and discussing public questions.
>
> Such use of the streets and public places has from ancient times, been a part of the privileges, immunities, rights, and liberties of citizens.

While most Justices didn't concur, subsequent opinions endorsed symbolic speech rights. In *Schneider v. State* (1939), the Court ruled that city ordinances to keep streets clean and presentable didn't justify prohibiting literature and leaflet distribution to willing recipients. In *Kunz v. New York* (1951), the Court held that mandating permits to speak publicly on religious issues was unconstitutional. In *Shuttlesworth v. City of Birmingham* (1969), the Court ruled for petitioner Shuttlesworth's right to lead orderly 1963 civil rights marches. Doing so had violated a city ordinance requiring permit permission. Calling it unconstitutional, the decision stated it was denied to censor ideas, not obstruct traffic.

Various High Court decisions ruled that speech, including camping out in public places, is subject to time, place and manner regulations such as traffic control. However, protected speech must have alternate ways to communicate without undue restrictions.

For example, in *Clark v. CCNV*, the Court ruled for the National Parks Service's right to prohibit camping out overnight because doing so complied with reasonable time, place and manner restrictions of expression. The Court said incidental speech restrictions are constitutional provided they're not greater than necessary to further a substantial governmental interest. However, it stressed that the restrictions must be narrowly tailored. That requirement is satisfied as long as it promotes a substantial governmental interest that would be achieved less effectively absent the regulation.[1]

Imposed restrictions must also be content neutral. The Court definedthree categories of public property and public right of use of same::

- streets and parks (considered a public forum), traditionally used for public assembly and debate; government may not prohibit communicative activity therein; moreover, content-neutral time, place, and manner restrictions must be justified to serve some legitimate interest;

- limited public forum space for use by certain groups, provided legitimate discriminatory limitations are justified by compelling government interests; and

- government "may reserve a forum for its intended purposes, communicative or otherwise, as long as the regulation on speech is reasonable and not an effort to suppress expression merely because public officials oppose the speaker's view."[2]

According to New York Mayor Michael Bloomberg, "The Constitution doesn't protect tents. It protects speech and assembly."[3] True or false?

It depends on whether legitimate concerns are justified, as well as other issues discussed above. Moreover, interpretations differ. Restrictions deemed proper by some may not be by others. Pace University Law Professor Bennett Gershman calls New York's tent city protected speech, saying that various Supreme Court cases affirmed that First Amendment protections aren't limited to speech and assembly. They also include "certain conduct that is intended to convey a message."[4]

New York's tent city resonated globally. As a result, Bloomberg wants it removed, despite its being "orderly and harmless." It doesn't "threaten public safety or traffic congestion." At most, sanitation concerns might be raised.

However, as Gershman noted, "protesters apparently are keeping things relatively clean and safe." Weighing "the right of individual expression...against the public interest in peace and quiet, the balance typically tilts toward free speech unless the government can demonstrate a substantial interest in curtailing the conduct, and also [shows that it's] not because of any disagreement with the content of the conduct-speech, but for some other legitimate government interest."[5]

Saying so isn't enough: you have to prove it conclusively. But Bloomberg didn't even try. Despite that, New York Supreme Court Justice Michael Stallman overruled Manhattan Supreme Court Justice Lucy Billings' restraining order in his favor. Billings had said protesters must be allowed back with "tents and other property." So far, they can come without tents and other belongings.

OWS lawyer Allan Levine argued that banning tents infringed First Amendment rights, saying: "The power of this symbolic speech is that it's a 24-hour occupation," replicated nationally. "This conveys a special message."[6]

Restricting First Amendment freedoms threatens all others even though guidelines regarding speech-related conduct aren't clear. Gershman said camping overnight in Central Park would differ markedly from doing so in Liberty Park Plaza (protesters call it Zuccotti Park). Moreover, its symbolic significance dramatically demonstrates "the economic disparities in our society without threatening any substantial public interest...." As a result, it's "well within" First Amendment parameters. Bloomberg should endorse, not condemn it."

Of course, Bloomberg and Wall Street are closely linked and the issue isn't public interest concerns, just his own and those of fellow Wall Street crooks. They want nothing interfering with their ability to manipulate world markets for profit, ripping off countries and people globally.

Real change isn't possible unless they are stopped. Accomplishing Job One opens all the other possibilities.

ENDNOTES

1   <http://supreme.justia.com/cases/federal/us/468/288/case.html#293>
2   Ibid.
3   < http://www.bloomberg.com/news/2011-10-17/wall-street-protesters-backed-3-to-1-by-new-yorkers-quinnipiac-poll-says.html>

4   <http://www.huffingtonpost.com/bennett-l-gershman/tent-city-is-protected-sp_b_1020822.html>

5   Ibid.

6   <http://articles.nydailynews.com/2011-11-16/news/30404589_1_tent-city-protesters-lawyers>

17

WASHINGTON TARGETS OWS

In October 2011, Obama told ABC News:

The most important thing we can do right now is those of us in leadership letting people know that we understand their struggles and we are on their side, and that we want to set up a system in which hard work, responsibility, doing what you're supposed to do, is rewarded...[1]

And that people who are irresponsible, who are reckless, who don't feel a sense of obligation to their communities and their companies and their workers that those folks aren't rewarded.

His key words were: "We are on their side."

At the same time, FBI, Department of Homeland Security (DHS), and Secret Service agents were working cooperatively with local authorities to infiltrate, disrupt, subvert, and destroy the Occupy Wall Street (OWS) movement in cities nationwide.

Celebratory hope accompanied Obama's election but after his campaign on a promise of hope and change, betrayal followed. He expanded the worst Bush policies, usurped and exercised unbridled powers.In June 2010, ACLU executive director Anthony Romero said Obama "disgusted" him. Civil liberty infringements worsened, and the rule of law faded.

As Yale Law Professor Jack Balkin said in 2011, "(w)e are witnessing the bipartisan normalization and legitimization of a national security state."[2] The Obama administration created a "parallel track of preventative law enforcement that bypasses traditional protections in the Bill of Rights."

In December 2008, before Obama took office, James Petras called him "the greatest con man in recent history,"[3] comparing him to Melville's Confidence Man. "He catches your eye while he picks your pocket." He promises one thing and delivers another consistently on issues mattering most.

A November 2008 Robert Fitch speech[4] to the Harlem Tenants Association revealed much about what lay ahead. He said Chicago urban planners yearned to make the city's south side developed like northern areas. They wanted to see demolitions for gentrification. Poor folks had to be driven out. Most were Black. As an Illinois state senator, Obama represented a targeted community. But his "core financial supporters" and "inmost circle of advisors" stood to profit from the process. "Obama's political base comes primarily from Chicago FIRE—finance, insurance and real estate industry" officials. Other key supporters included liberal foundations, elite universities, NGO community developers, and "real estate reverends who (preach and) produce market rate housing" at the expense of poor people who are kicked out for the aforementioned beneficiaries.Altogether, Fitch called it "Friendly FIRE... disguised by the camouflage of community uplift, augmented by the authority of academia, greased by billions in foundation grants, and wired" to provisions of the Community Reinvestment Act of 1995

Obama was their guy, a front man. As president, Chicago-style hope and change was repeated across America. Before Obama taking office in January 2009, Fitch saw what lay ahead. He wasn't alone. The Partnership for Civil Justice Fund (PCJF) is a public service legal organization. It's "Dedicated to Defending Democracy in the Courts... and in the Streets"[5]—the defense of human and civil rights secured by law, the protection of free speech and dissent, and the elimination of prejudice and discrimination. Among the PCJF cases are constitutional law, civil rights, women's rights, economic justice matters and Freedom of Information Act cases.Its work includes "landmark constitutional rights litigation, often concentrated in the areas of free speech, assembly or other protected political organizing activity." According to PCJF's executive director, Mara Verheyden-Hilliard:

> The major defining feature of the Obama administration
> on (core constitutional issues) is the eagerness with
> which it embraced the stunning evisceration of civil
> rights and liberties that was a hallmark of the Bush

administration, and then deepened those outrageous programs. He has successfully counted on the acquiescent silence of the liberals.

In March, 2012, PCJF obtained heavily redacted Freedom of Information Act (FOIA) requested documents. They showed federal agencies began "coordinated intelligence gathering and operations on"[6] OWS last September.

On September 17, 2011, protests began in New York's Zuccotti Park. Secret Service agents were there covertly. The Department of Homeland Security (DHS) was also involved.Documents show its top officials "were preoccupied with the Occupy movement and have gone out of their way to project the appearance of an absence of federal involvement in the monitoring of and crackdown on Occupy."

"On the street it would be called 'Three Card Monte,' a swindler's game to hide the ball—a game of misdirection. The House always wins."

Before Zuccotti Park's first demonstration, the DHS Office of Intelligence and Analysis (I&A) prepared National Cybersecurity and Communications Integration (NCCIC) alerts about planned OWS demonstrations.

Since 9/11, America has become a total surveillance society. Millions are covertly watched. Their communications are monitored, including phone calls, emails, and other online activity. This ongoing spying alerted authorities to upcoming OWS plans. They were ready well in advance.

In response to FOIA, press, and public inquiries of its involvement, one DHS official wrote:

> I understand we have already received some FOIA requests regarding our possible reporting of the 'Occupy'....protests.
>
> I think should the FOIA experts find it appropriate to release information about the manner in which this issue was managed with DHS, it could only be perceived as a positive by those in the public who closely (observe) the Department.

DHS tried to evade and obstruct a complete FOIA search to conceal its disruptive and coordinated activities with other federal agencies and local authorities.

On April 30, 2012 PCJF "updated and made public the largest and most comprehensive" ever FOIA-obtained DC police documents obtained after years of hard fought litigation. Washington police operate under a "cloak of secrecy." Sunshine revealed some of what it conceals.Society's most disadvantaged are harmed across America. DC is a microcosm of authoritarian police serving powerful interests at the expense of ordinary people. Willful legal violations occur. No one's held accountable. Anyone challenging the system is targeted.

In part, PCJF cracked the District of Columbia government's wall of secrecy, obtaining a trove of materials and making them public. PCJF called their acquisition "historic."On May 3, 2012, it headlined, "DHS Releases More Documents on Occupy to PCJF." They reveal "massive (federal) nationwide" OWS monitoring and information sharing between DHS and local authorities.According to Verheyden-Hilliard:

> These documents show not only intense government monitoring and coordination in response to the Occupy Movement, but reveal a glimpse into the interior of a vast, tentacled, national intelligence and domestic spying network that the US government operates against its own people...

"These heavily redacted documents don't tell the full story. They are likely only a subset of responsive materials and the PCJF continues to fight for a complete release," she stated. "They scratch the surface of a mass intelligence network" apparatus operating against the interests of ordinary Americans.

The acquired documents reveal "intense" federal monitoring of OWS activities including names, addresses, and other relevant information of those involved. NORTHCOM is kept informed ahead of planned demonstrations.

DHS stays in direct communication with the White House regarding ongoing operations and approved "public statements denying DHS's involvement in Occupy actions."DHS Secretary Janet Napolitano runs its anti-OWS operations along with FBI and other federal agency officials. Obama appointed her.

The man who told ABC News "we are on their side," in fact oversees a plan to disrupt, subvert, and destroy what they're working for.

ENDNOTES

1   <http://abcnews.go.com/blogs/politics/2011/10/obama-occupy-wall-street-not-that-different-from-tea-party-protests/>

2   < http://www.salon.com/2012/04/20/obamas_dismal_civil_liberties_record/>

3   James Petras, *Global Depression and Regional Wars*, Clarity Press, Inc., 2010, pp. 49-56.

4   < http://www.scribd.com/doc/92392289/Fitch-on-Obama>

5   < http://www.justiceonline.org/index.html>

6   < http://www.justiceonline.org/commentary/dhs.html>

18

TARGETING JOURNALISTS COVERING OWS PROTESTS

On September, 17, 2011, US DayofRage.org organized protests in New York, Los Angeles, San Francisco, Portland, OR, and Austin, TX. They hoped many more would follow, grow, and spread nationwide. Indeed, they already had—to over 1,000 large and small cities, towns, and communities. "We have had enough," the protesters said. "Help us reclaim democracy."

Currently, many social justice issues drive them to take to the streets. And when they do, police violence confronts them. Oakland Mayor Jean Quan admitted coordinating crackdown efforts with counterparts in other cities. Examiner.com reporter Rick Ellis said an anonymous federal official told him that "in several [late 2011] conference calls and briefings, local police agencies were advised to seek a legal reason to evict residents of tent cities, focusing on zoning laws and existing curfew rules."[1] They were also "advised to demonstrate a massive show of police force, including large numbers in riot gear."

Last October 2011, Obama duplicitously said, "[W]e are on their side." The side of the protesters, he implied, but it was just another statement that proved he is a serial liar, since in actuality, his policies solely support wealth, power, and imperial dominance. The Nobel Laureat/Harvard professor of constitutional law has disregarded rule of law principles, democratic values, and social justice. While he's ravaging the world one country at a time, he's also waging war at home against dissent. His new National Defense Authorization Act—an indefinite military detention law—targets OWS, other like-minded activists, and anyone threatening US hegemony.

Washington began aiding cities' efforts to confront OWS protesters violently even before NDAA passed. FBI officials are involved in determining the appropriate tactics and perhaps even directly. (Federal and undercover police provocateurs often disrupt public protests violently.) They advised that evictions be conducted late at night or in the pre-dawn when local press coverage is absent or minimal.

Department of Defense training manuals call protests "low-level terrorism." An *FBI memo* says peace protesters are "terrorists." Throughout his tenure, Obama's been more active destroying human rights and civil liberties than Bush II.

Journalists are singled out and targeted. On January 7, 2012, Press TV said nearly 40 journalists have been arrested since September protests began. In early January, technicians working for Global Revolution were arrested for streaming live OWS protest video.[2] Homeland Security's Federal Protective Service arrested an Occupy Portland photographer.

Journalists have been harassed, arrested, handcuffed, and beaten for doing their job. Free Press.net's Journalism and Public Media Campaign Director Josh Stearns[3] reported in November 2011 that 10 New York-based journalists were violently arrested in an early morning raid. They were trying to cover Zuccotti Park evictions. Police accused them of trespassing. They all had valid NYPD-issued press passes.

In response, New York-based journalists formed the Coalition for the First Amendment.[4] It consists of 13 membership organizations representing mainly New York City journalists.

International Press Institute (IPI) executive director Alison Bethel McKenzie said:

> This attempt by New York City authorities to hinder the work of journalists reporting on a matter of vital public interest is completely unacceptable. Journalists must be allowed to operate in a climate free from harassment and intimidation—and above all, free from the use of violence. We insist that the NYPD respect the rights of all members of the media, who play an essential role in a health democracy.[5]

IPI, other groups, and First Amendment advocates expressed concern about similar confrontations nationally. Earlier, IPI had reported journalist arrests in Oakland, Milwaukee, Tennessee, and student journalists in Atlanta.

Concerned New York Press Club members got involved. They're now monitoring police/press relations on constitutional rights issues. On

November 15, 2011, in an open letter to Mayor Michael Bloomberg and Police Commissioner Raymond Kelly, they protested police harassment and arrests of reporters covering OWS protests. They urged investigations and assurances that these practices will end. Despite that, police violent actions continue against protesters, journalists, and others nearby.

Mayor Bloomberg disingenuously defends police action, saying it's done "to protect members of the press." He also accused protesters of "deliberately pursu(ing) violence." But in actuality, the demonstrators are entirely peaceful, even when rogue cops beat them.

Nonetheless, Bloomberg claimed police "maintained incredible restraint" despite video and witness confirmation of brutality to the contrary. Police Commissioner Kelly indicated future arrests would be handled the same way. In response, Manhattan Borough President Scott Stringer strongly condemned police actions, calling them "outrageous." and saying "Zuccotti Park is not Tiananmen Square."

First Amendment Coalition (FAC) Activism

Founded in 1988 as the California First Amendment Coalition[6], FAC later went national. It's "dedicated to advancing free speech, more open and accountable government, and public participation in civic affairs."

FAC's activities include:

- free legal help for journalists, activists, academics, and others on First Amendment issues;

- "strategic litigation" for First Amendment rights;

- educational and informational efforts through conferences, books, and online material;

- "legislative oversight of bills affecting access to government; and

- public advocacy through" op-eds and public appearances.

Police Brutality 101

On November 25, 2011, Naomi Wolf's London *Guardian* article headlined, "The shocking truth about the crackdown on Occupy,"[7] saying thatOWS protesters and journalists faced "unparallelled police brutality" in coordinated nationwide crackdowns. Militarized cops in riot gear beat, pepper-sprayed, and otherwise harmed nonviolent men and women, young and old, workers and unemployed, veterans and opposing off-duty police, and others joining them seeking social justice.

"The National Union of Journalists [filed] a Freedom of Information Act (FOIA) request to investigate possible federal involvement," including efforts targeting journalists.

On November 21, 2011, even *New York Times* writer Michael Powell commented in his article titled, "Reporters Meet the Fists of the Law," saying "Over several days, New York cops have arrested, punched, whacked, shoved to the ground and tossed a barrier at reporters and photographers."[8] Not only that:

> My *Times* colleague Colin Moynihan stood on that darkened square last Tuesday morning when a police spokesman shouted, "Who has press credentials?" Many reporters and photographers dutifully raised their hands. With that, the police removed the "credentialed" reporters, under threat of arrest, to a press pen, out of sight of the square.

While taking notes, AP and *Daily News* reporters were arrested. So was a radio reporter recording material near Zuccotti Park. Post-9/11, Powell continues, "police have grown accustomed to forcibly penning, arresting, and sometimes spraying and whacking protesters and reporters." In one of many incidents, police assaulted a photographer for doing his job. They "ran at him, grabbed (a) barrier and struck him in the chest, knees, and shins."[9] Similar violence now occurs nationwide. Protesters, journalists, and even public officials and distinguished figures are affected.

In mid-November, rogue cops violently shoved New York Supreme Court Justice Karen Smith against a wall. She represented the National Lawyers Guild as a legal observer. She had intervened to stop a mother from being beaten. For her efforts, she was assaulted. A New York City council member was also beaten, and in Berkeley, CA, police assaulted former US Poet Laureate Robert Hass with batons.

On January 2, 2012, *New York Times* writer Powell again commented in an article headlined, "The Rules on News Coverage Are Clear, but the Police Keep Pushing,"[10] that NYPD assaults on journalists continue, citing Reporter Ryan Devereaux as "Exhibit 1A that all is not well. On Dec. 17," he covered a Duarte Square protest. "A linebacker-size officer grabbed (his) collar." His visible ID identified him as a reporter. Nonetheless, "(t)he cop jammed a fist into his throat, turning (him) into a de facto battering ram to push back protesters." Devereaux yelled "I'm a journalist." The cop yelled "Push, boys!" Brutality it continued. An AP photographer captured it. On New Year's eve, "a (police) captain began pushing Colin Moynihan," another *New York Times* reporter. When he complained, he was threatened with losing his press credentials.

A Final Comment

First Amendment rights and local regulations are clear. Civil liberties lawyer Norman Siegel, State Senator Eric Adams, and two others wrote Commissioner Kelly, saying what the law requires: "The media will be given access as close to the activity as possible, with a clear line of sight and within hearing range of the incident."

Instead, police assault and prevent reporters from doing their job. Mayoral press representatives claim the police are acting responsibly. One spokesman even told Powell: "It is impossible to say the reporters were not breaking the law." In fact, reporters *were* doing their job responsibly. According to Senator Adams who's also a retired police captain: "If the police and the mayor won't" observe First Amendment rights and "follow their own rules, whose rules will they follow?"

Who will defend private citizens, including journalists, when federal and city officials abuse them?

Unless social justice protests continue America's headed for full-blown tyranny.

ENDNOTES

1. <http://www.examiner.com/article/update-occupy-crackdowns-coordinated-with-federal-law-enforcement-officials>
2. < http://www.presstv.ir/detail/219738.html>
3. < http://www.fair.org/blog/2011/11/16/crackdown-on-journalists-at-occupy-wall-street/>
4. < http://www.newyorkpressclub.org/coalition.php>
5. < http://www.trust.org/trustmedia/news/ipi-journalists-arrested-across-the-us/>
6. < http://www.firstamendmentcoalition.org/>
7. < http://www.guardian.co.uk/commentisfree/cifamerica/2011/nov/25/shocking-truth-about-crackdown-occupy>
8. < http://www.nytimes.com/2011/11/22/nyregion/nypd-stops-reporters-with-badges-and-fists.html?_r=1>
9. Ibid.
10. < http://www.nytimes.com/2012/01/03/nyregion/at-wall-street-protests-clash-of-reporting-and-policing.html?ref=gotham>

19

SOCIAL JUSTICE ON TRIAL IN CANADA

Canada's conservative government force-feeds Canadians the same kind of destructive neoliberal policies that are harming American and European societies. They include wage and benefit cuts, less social spending, privatization of state resources, mass layoffs, deregulation, tax cuts for corporations and super-rich elites, harsh crackdowns against resisters and sharp hikes to college tuition fees.

In the 1980s, this policy regimen was called Reaganomics, trickle down, and Thatcherism. In the 1990s, it was "shock therapy." Today, it's austerity. The result is unprecedented wealth transfers to corporate favorites and privileged elites. Capital's divine rights are prioritized while social justice is on the chopping block for elimination. Living standards are sacrificed. Ordinary people lose out as vital services are cut. Human needs go begging. Unemployment and poverty soar. So does rage for change.

Years ago Canada lost its moorings. In December 1984, Conservative Prime Minister Brian Mulroney addressed these policies that had begun elsewhere in the 1970s. Speaking before the New York Economic Club, he announced: "Canada is open for business."He meant US companies were welcome. Both countries cooperated to achieve greater economic integration. Corporate interests were prioritized. Ordinary people lost out.

"Oh Canada" (the national anthem) took on new meaning as sacrificing pluralist Canadian democracy and social justice traditions became policy. Major parties formed a consensus the same way that Democrats and Republicans do in America. Neoliberal harshness was institutionalized. The conservative Harper government stiffened earlier policies serving Canada's ruling class. Finance capital is dominant. What big money wants it gets. Corporate power overall makes policy.

Canada had shifted hard right under Mulroney. Harper institutionalized it further. In January 2012, he addressed Davos World Economic Forum participants pledging "transformative" pro-business policies including more tax cuts, privatizations, deregulation, and austerity hitting ordinary people hardest. "We will do more, much more," he promised.

Social Canada was hardest hit. In March 2012, Canada's House of Commons passed budget cuts and austerity measures eliminating thousands of public sector jobs, cutting billions from federal programs, raising the retirement age to 67, and calling federal debt the problem to be addressed. It was the same canard America and European countries have used to justify harsh neoliberal policies.

Canadian social justice is following the same downward trajectory as in America and across Europe, en route to being eliminated altogether. Higher education is affected. Once it was affordable. It no longer is for many as tuition and fees soar.

Last winter, Quebec's Liberal government announced tuition fee increases over the next five years of around 75% (or $1,625). Thousands of students reacted. In mid-February, protests and strikes began. One of three provincial student associations initiated them: the Coalition large de l'association pour une solidarite syndicale etudiante (CLASSE: the Broader Coalition of the Association of Student-Union Solidarity). Others joined in: FEUQ (the Quebec Federation of University Students) and FECQ (Quebec Federation of College Students).

Thousands swelled to 200,000 or more. Most Quebecers supported them. Sharp tuition and fee increases were forcing students and families into debtwhile others were dropping out. Available aid is meager compared to years earlier, making higher education more and more unaffordable.

When the students' reaction by strikes and protests continued into their fourth month, they were confronted by the police. Clashes and arrests follow—the usual pattern against all social justice demonstrations. Legitimate struggles are criminalized.

Criminalizing dissent became policy. On May 18, Quebec's Liberal government passed Bill 78 prohibiting student protests or any other "formof gathering" within 50 meters of the "outer limits" of the "grounds" of any university or CEGEP (College of general and vocational education) building.

In Quebec, high school ends at grade 11. Completing CEGEP grades 12 and 13 is required for college or university admission. Doing it successfully earns students DECs (diplômes d›études collegial). CEGEPs also offer three-year programs in vocational studies, computer science, nursing, and other fields. With DEC credits, Bachelor›s degrees can be completed in three years. Supporters and critics disagree on the system›s merits or disadvantages. It›s unique to Quebec.

Bill 78 also requires student associations, unions representing teachers, and CEGEP staff to «employ appropriate means to induce» compliance with enacted measures or face prosecution. Article 9 authorizes the Minister of Education, Recreation and Sports to modify any law to ensure school sessions throughout the bill›s time frame. All demonstrations exceeding 50 people were declared illegal without provincial police approval. Offenders faced daily fines. A date for education employees to return to work was established. Winter semester classes at 11 universities and 14 CEGEPs were suspended. Completing them by August or September was mandated.

The law was set to expire July 1, 2013. It›s patently illegal. The 1982 Constitution Act established the Constitution of Canada. It contains a bill of rights called *The Charter of Rights and Freedoms*, which states everyone has the following fundamental freedoms:

(a) freedom of conscience and religion;

(b) freedom of thought, belief, opinion and expression, including freedom of the press and other media of communication;

(c) freedom of peaceful assembly; and

(d) freedom of association.

Article 7 assures that "Everyone has the right to life, liberty and security of person and the right not to be deprived thereof in accordance with the principles of fundamental justice."

Academic and speech freedoms are fundamental in free societies. So are public assembly and association rights. Without them, all others are threatened. Howard Zinn called dissent "the highest form of patriotism." Voltaire said, "I may disapprove of what you say, but I will defend to the death your right to say it." Jefferson said, "The spirit of resistance to government is so valuable on certain occasions that I wish it to be always kept alive."

But Bill 78 violates Canada's Charter of Rights and Freedoms. So does a newly passed Montreal City Council ordinance criminalizing face paint, niqabs, and other face or head coverings while demonstrating.

On May 22, 2012, it was invoked. Baton-wielding police confronted downtown Montreal protesters violently,using tear gas and arresting dozens. Charges claimed protesters wore illegal masks and/or confronted police violently.

On May 21, confrontations occurred in Sherbrooke. It's Quebec Premier Jean Charest's home city. Dozens of arrests followed. Charges included demonstrating illegally.

A Final Comment

Sustained activism works. Victories come in small steps. They all matter. Last spring, anti-austerity protests erupted. Striking students got little support but persisted. It paid off. On September 4, the Parti Quebecois (PQ) won 54 of 125 National Assembly seats in provincial elections. It was enough to put it in power heading a minority government and ending nine years of Liberal Party rule. On September 20, the PQ rescinded tuition increases.

Government officials plan an education summit later this year or early 2013. Quebec Premier Pauline Marois advocates indexing tuition to inflation. Students oppose any increases. One student group, CLASSE, wants tuition-free higher education. Others don't rule out more protests if tuition isn't permanently frozen.

Like other Western societies, Canada supports neoliberal harshness, eroding social programs for years. What's ahead bears watching. Dominant Conservatives and Liberals aren't people-friendly. The PQ may follow their agenda in Quebec.

Affordable education is vital. So are all social justice rights. They're too important to sacrifice. Committed opposition is needed to stop force-fed austerity.

Students and workers must bond. They're largely on their own. Together, their chance for social justice improves. Union officials sold out to power. Who knows where this ends.

Class war rages in Canada and other Western societies where governments serve wealth and power interests only. People's needs suffer. Ordinary people face neo-serfdom, debt peonage, and police state repression for fighting back, but it's their only chance for change.

A protracted struggle remains ahead. In fact, it's just begun. Staying the course is key. All great victories come in baby steps. They're never achieved easily or quickly. Hopefully Quebec students and workers understand today's reality. They're on their own to save rights that are too important to lose.

20

FRENCH WORKERS' STRUGGLES FOR JUSTICE

During October 2010, France resembled France of May 1968. Predatory capitalism went on trial. More on that below. The issue over ten decades later was austerity measures and exasperation with Sarkozy's government which blatantly favored super-rich elites over popular interests. Sarkozy was elected on the slogan, "Work more to earn more," but today's reality is work harder to earn less. Like in America, public coffers are emptied for super-rich elites. People suffer to pay bankers. In contrast, post-WW II social security benefits are being dismantled in real time on the pretext that France can't afford it.

Wealth is being systematically transferred like in America and throughout Europe when ailing economies need massive stimulus to spur growth and create jobs.Instead, only capital, investments, and the ability to compete are addressed. Neoliberal austerity is demanded. Stressed households are asked for more sacrifices. They know it, and protest through strikes, street demonstrations, and other actions.

As in America and across Europe, high finance rules. Wage and benefit cuts as well as deindustrialization follow. As a result, production moves offshore to cheap labor markets. High-paying jobs disappear, and with them a former way of life.

France needs to complete the popular actions that almost succeeded in 1968. Even then, French unions backed government power, not their rank and file. In his 1970 book, *Prelude to Revolution: France in May 1968*, Daniel Singer asked if a "socialist revolution" was beginning, and whether "Marxism [was] returning to its home ground, the advanced countries for which it was designed?" Indeed, he believed that was so, calling the May uprising "a revolutionary situation [that] can occur in [any] advanced capitalist country."

It began with student revolts in Germany, Italy, Japan, Mexico, America, France, and elsewhere with the potential for much more. It was the biggest working class eruption since the 1930s. At its peak, 10 million joined students and other protesters. They went on strike, occupied factories, universities, and offices throughout the country. They paralyzed it, and nearly ousted de Gaulle's government, which was unable to counter the most profound challenge to capitalism since the 30s and 1917 Russia.

For weeks, direct worker actions in factories and other takeovers continued. "Dual power" was created—tthe government v. revolutionary action committees. Workers wanted democratic reforms, "including industrial democracy, that does not just rest on an occasional ballot." Their actions "precipitated the biggest general strike in French history, paralyzing the economy and raising, for a brief spell, the question of power in the country."

Capitalism was on trial. Transitioning to socialism was possible. Under the slogan, "Be realistic, demand the impossible!" it could have gone either way.. Singer believed workers had a chance to take over "a share of the management and then [expand] to full management by collective producers." His model embraced two characteristics:

- students acting before or independently from workers; then

- workers joining ranks in support, united against a common enemy, turning rebellion into "potential revolution."

Singer understood that "workers [couldn't] conquer economic power under capitalism as the bourgeoisie did under feudalism." Their task is harder, but he saw in France the potential for change where working class people acted "in parallel" to achieve it.

Years later, Singer said a better future depends on "structural reforms" or "revolutionary reformism," the kind now needed more than ever . Perhaps street protests across Europe and OWS in America have potential and staying power to achieve it.But today, hardline governments oppose them unlike in 1968 when governments made political and social concessions to retain power. Years later the concessions were lost under Thatcher in Britain, Kohl in Germany and Reagan in Americawho began a three decade assault on working class wages, benefits and values. Clinton, Bush II, Obama, and their European counterparts intensified it.

In 1968 France, revolutionary change was possible. The nation was paralyzed, the government powerless. Trade unions lost control of their workers, who had enough strength to take over. It didn't happen because the supposedly revolutionary French Communist Party (PCF), its union ally, the Confederation general du travail (CGT), as well as the Fourth International Trotskyist Pabloite United Secretariat, and its French branches allied to stop it.

Events unfolded as follows. In January, student protests began. At first small, they got larger, then they spread from one city to another. In Caen, Bordeaux, and elsewhere, workers and students massed on streets. On April 12, 1968, solidarity Paris protests supported German student leader Rudi Dutschke after a right-wing hooligan shot him in Berlin. In March, students occupied the University of Nanterre's administration building. The Paris Sorbonne was then targeted.

On May 3, as student leaders planned their next moves, police responded, clearing the campus disruptively. Students, in return, erected barricades. Arrests followed. The Communist Party opposed student activists. Its second in command leader, George Marchais, called them "fascist provocateurs" but failed to subdue the movement. Events gained traction on their own. Protests grew and spread nationwide.

On May 8, a one-day western France strike took place. On May 10 and 11, the "Night of the Barricades" engulfed the Latin Quarter of Paris. Thousands of students erected barricades in the university district. Police stormed them late at night. Hundreds were injured, many arrested as Prime Minister George Pompidou reopened the Sorbonne. Students being held in custody were released. Then on May 13 a general strike was called against police repression.

A huge response followed, the largest mass uprising since WW II. In Paris alone, 800,000 filled the streets. Political demands included toppling the government—regime change. The Sorbonne and other universities were again occupied. Trade unions tried to limit the strike action to one day, but failed. On May 14, workers occupied the Nantes Sud-Aviation factory. They held it for a month.

Across France, from May 15-20, hundreds of other occupations followed, including at the country's largest factory, the Billancourt Renault plant. Many of its managers were held captive. Worker/action committees demanded higher wages and benefits, shorter working hours, no recriminations, and more worker rights, overall.

By May 20, all France was shut down. A general strike paralyzed the country, without calls from trade unions or other organizations. Nonetheless, everywhere, factories, offices, universities and schools were occupied. Production, commerce, transport and education were halted. Ten million workers participated, two-thirds of the workforce. It was the most massive strike in French history.

From May 22-30, events peaked, but continued into July. According to the French Labor Ministry, 150 million working days were lost. It was an astonishing number compared to other similar, but smaller, actions.

By late May, the de Gaulle government had lost control. Demands for its resignation grew. On May 24, de Gaulle addressed the nation on national television. He promised referendum reforms, giving workers and students more rights. He had no impact whatever. Had workers and students kept up the pressure for weeks longer, they might not only have brought de Gaulle down but also changed France.

It was a historic moment for revolutionary change—but it didn't happen. The Communist Party/General Confederation of Labor andaffiliated groups' collaboration prevented it, saving the Fifth Republic.

Only modest concessions were granted. Smaller strikes and occupations continued for weeks, and years passed before calm entirely returned. Two months after the strikes began, the elitites regained power. They bought time and used it effectively to solidify control against waning revolutionary zeal.

A Final Comment

Years later, Singer said the following: People understand we're "living in an oppressive and unjust society. Only they think there is no way out. [We're] now told that capitalism—ccall it hell, paradise, or purgatory— is the one system from which there is no possible way outThe great success of our huge propaganda machine [is in having] spread the conviction that" there's no alternative. Britain's Margaret Thatcher called it TINA. She lied, but as elitists know, their power depends on "our acceptance, our resignation."

Popular pundits, preachers and governments "doom as impossible a radical, fundamental transformation of existing society." No matter that it would be infinitely better than today's. Open discussions about it are suppressed.

No matter. Recall the French slogan, "Be realistic, Ask for the Impossible." It exhorts us to "recover the conviction that we can change life, *changez la vie*, through collective political action. When that conviction" gains critical mass, "all the establishments will once again begin to tremble." They'll know change is coming. The "impossible" indeed is reachable when enough determined people seize it.

What better time than now when revolutionary change is needed to counter destructive government policies?

21

"GRAND BARGAIN" BETRAYAL COMING

Obama's economic record includes nearly 25 million unemployed, around 23% of working age Americans without jobs, poverty, homelessness, and hunger at record levels or close to it, and the greatest wealth disparity in US history.

Privileged elites have benefitted enormously on his watch and will get plenty more, ahead. Bipartisan complicity will lead Congress to make things worse, not better. Huge budget cuts loom, with social programs to be hit hardest.

America's compromised progressive left hailed Obama's victorywhen it should condemned both Obama and the fraudulent Congressional process. *The Nation* magazine lost its soul long ago. Throughout its history, it pretended to stand for social justice, but in actuality, it scorns truth and turns reality on its head. It ducks responsible reporting on issues that matter most.

Accordingly, on November 7, 2012, it headlined "A Progressive Surge,"[1] saying:

> While President Obama's re-election inspires varying degrees of hope among progressives, it has evoked one common sentiment: relief. Democracy may not be reborn, but a living symbol of plutocracy was defeated by the voters on November 6.

It's hard to believe so-called progressive editors would publish such outrageous rubbish. Obama matches Romney's anti-populist agenda blow for blow. They agree on almost everything benefitting corporate favorites and rich elites at the expense of all others. They scorn social America and don't give a damn about people needs. To pretend otherwise is unprincipled, reprehensible, and stupid.

Nonetheless, *Nation* editors celebrated "exhilarating wins" for Obama and likeminded Democrats. Hail to the other party of the rich. America's duopoly calls progressivism a four-letter word—*dead*. "We are glad the 1 percent (was) rebuffed at the polls," *Nation* editors prattled on… "We are glad that progressive politics … made the difference."

Perhaps they meant Venezuela's election, where in October, people power defeated privilege. Letting Obama lead America's second Big Money Party for another four years assures worse for ordinary people than in term one. It's baked in the cake.

Too bad *Nation* readers were deceived, just like regular *New York Times* adherents. On November 7, the NYT editorial headlined "An Invigorated Second Term," saying "Without question, (Obama) intends to build on and improve the significant accomplishments of the last four years….to keep the economy growing."[2]

Obama's first term record was enough to make some despots blush. His economic policies are weapons of mass destruction affecting ordinary people. He's got further mass immiseration in mind for term two. He also plans more war on humanity globally. *Times* editors want his mandate used to "broaden his agenda." How much more scorched earth hell can people stand? They'll shortly find out straightaway.

The top domestic policy is massive social benefit cuts. Newspeak terminology has substituted "grand bargain" for "austerity." "Fiscal cliff" language refers to expiring yearend tax breaks and unemployment benefits, as well as looming $1.2 trillion in largely discretionary sequestered cuts to address them, as mandated by the 2011 *Budget Control Act*. Automatic reductions will affect vital social programs. Medicare, Medicaid, public pensions, food stamps, and other important ones will be hit hard. But the sequestered $1.2 trillion is just for starters. Around $4 trillion over the next decade has been agreed on. It isn't about deficit cutting, it's about protecting corporate handouts and Bush era tax cuts, as well as expanding them for business and upper-bracket earners.

Bush era tax cuts cost America at least $3.5 trillion in vital revenue. Important domestic needs were sacrificed to make them possible. If they are maintained or increased for 10 more years, another $3.5 trillion or more will be lost. At the same, deficits will rise. Even conservative projections show it. More realistic ones reveal ominous numbers.

America's duopoly has already agreed on cuts and increases in principle. When publicly announced, newspeak duplicity will conceal the severity of what's coming, with initial cuts expected on January 1, 2013 or shortly thereafter.

From post-election November 2012 through yearend, four major issues must be resolved:

(1) Extending the 2% payroll tax deduction another year. This is a stealth drain of hundreds of billions of dollars from Social Security's Trust Fund reserves. The revenue already lost has irreparably weakened its ability to pay future benefits. If it loses more the entire program may be lost. Privatization assures it. Obama fully concurs on driving a stake through the heart of Medicare, Medicaid, Social Security and public pensions. He's no progressive. He's a corporatist hardliner. Otherwise, he never would have become president otherwise. Populists needn't apply.

(2) Extending expiring unemployment benefits for millions of laid off workers.

(3) Another one-year Alternative Minimum Tax (AMT) fix.

(4) Delaying the 29% cut in doctors' fees for serving Medicare patients.

Expect Republicans to drive a hard bargain like they always do. Democrats pretend they careand are fighting it, when in fact, they've already sold out. Obama's reelection hinged on it. He talks tough, then caves at the 11th hour. He did so repeatedly throughout his first term.

People needs don't matter. It's part of a longstanding plan to Third Worldize America.

On November 6, 2012, Bill Black discussed what's coming. His article headlined "Wall Street Urges Obama to Commit the Great Betrayal," pointing out that the top domestic policy is eroding safety net protections en route to eliminating them altogether.

> Only a Democrat can make it politically safe for Republicans who hate the safety net to unravel it (a process that would occur over a number of years) by legitimizing the claim that (it) must be cut.[3]

Obama was hand-picked to do it, since "Republicans have been unable to deliver Wall Street's unholy grail —privatizing Social Security." Doing so will let financial predators

> charge tens of billions of dollars in fees annually and the banks that administered the privatized program would be systemically dangerous institutions (SDIs) because the consequences of allowing bank failures to cause tens of millions of Americans to lose their retirement savings would require either that all such deposits be federally insured or that the failing banks be bailed out by the federal government...

Privatization, therefore, is a convenient fiction. The
banks' profits will be privatized. Any catastrophic losses
will be borne by the public.

The Big Lie claims no acceptable alternative exists. Safety net
cuts must be imposed. Obama's knife is a sharpened dagger at the heart of
what matters most to ordinary people. Their welfare, security and futures
are up for grabs. They're being destroyed in plain sight, even as the so-
called progressives hail "four more years."

Force-fed austerity assures the worst of hard times. It's
responsible for what Black calls "the four horsemen of the economic
apocalypse:"

- economic decline;

- job cuts and greater unemployment;

- increased deficits and debt; and

- destruction of safety net protections.

Combined, they assure third world status. Black said Obama
prioritizes it. We're forewarned but does it matter? Few Americans even
understand what's coming. A "grand bargain" betrayal is planned. It will
come in stages like boiling a frog which doesn't know it's dinner until
too late. Standard & Poor's and other rating agencies endorse it. They're
corporate tools, mostly representing Wall Street and other financial
interests. S&P's marching orders called for downgrading US credit to
AA+. So it did so in August 2011, saying:

> The markets have spoken and anyone who continues
> to insist that entitlements or taxes are off the table is
> condemning the US to second rate economic status and
> a permanent downgrade.
>
> America's credit rating is at a crossroads. We can
> choose to heed this message by finishing the deficit
> reduction job with a balanced plan that is composed
> mainly of entitlement cuts, closing tax loopholes and
> defense cuts, or we can squabble while our global
> standing continues to sink.
>
> The markets have spoken and anyone who
> continues to insist that entitlements or taxes are off the

table is condemning the US to second rate economic status and a permanent downgrade.

The S&P statement targeted safety net protections. Including defense and tax loopholes merely reflected a pro forma deception..You can expect fast and loose deception to conceal what's really going on. Obama's an old hand at it. As James Petras pointed out even before his first election, he's a con man. But he's Wall Street's man. They chose him and expect four more years of subservience. He won't disappoint. Throughout his political career, Obama's been a stealth Republican. His voting record proves it. Reelecting him serves elitist interests well.

They know what they want and now they've got it.

ENDNOTES

1   <http://www.thenation.com/article/171102/progressive-surge?rel=email>

2   <http://www.nytimes.com/2012/11/08/opinion/an-invigorated-second-term-for-president-obama.html?_r=2&>

3   <http://www.nakedcapitalism.com/2012/11/bill-black-wall-street-urges-obama-to-commit-the-great-betrayal.html>

22

LEGISLATING TYRANNY IN AMERICA

Obama won't prosecute CIA torturers, Wall Street crooks, other corporate criminals, lawless war profiteers, or other venal high-level civilian or government officials. In contrast, he endorsed indefinite military detentions of US citizens allegedly associated with terrorist groups, with or without corroborating evidence.

Post-9/11, US freedoms and other democratic values have been dramatically eroded. The enactment of police state provisions in the FY 2012 *National Defense Authorization Act* (NDAA) comes closer to ending them entirely. More on it below, but first:

The October 17, 2006 Bush enactment of the *Military Commissions Act* authorized torture and gave government sweeping unconstitutional powers to detain, interrogate, and prosecute alleged suspects and collaborators (including US citizens), hold them (without evidence) indefinitely in military prisons, and deny them habeas and other constitutional protections.

Section 1031 of the FY 2010 *Defense Authorization Act* contained the 2009 Military Commissions Act (MCA). The phrase "unprivileged enemy belligerent" replaced "unlawful enemy combatant."

The language changed but not the intent or its essential lawlessness. Obama embraced the Bush agenda, including keeping Guantanamo open after promising to close it, allowing torture there and abroad, and treating US citizens as lawlessly as the US treats foreign nationals.

The MCA grants sweeping police state powers, including protecting MCA prerogatives from interference by American courts. It stipulates that "no court, justice, or judge shall have jurisdiction to hear or consider any claim or cause for action whatsoever... relating to the prosecution, trial, or judgment of a military commission [including] challenges to the lawfulness of [its] procedures...."

The MCA scraped habeas protection (an historic human advance dating back to the 1215 Magna Carta that is lauded in the schoolbooks of American children) for domestic and foreign state enemies, citizens and non-citizens alike. It says "Any person is punishable... who... aids, abets, counsels, commands, or procures," and in so doing helps a foreign enemy, provide "material support" to alleged terrorist groups, engages in spying, or commits other offenses previously handled in civil courts. No evidence is needed. Those charged are guilty by accusation.

Other key provisions include:

• legalizing torture against anyone, letting the president decide what procedures can be used on his own authority;

• denying detainees international law protection;

• letting the executive interpret or ignore international and US law;

• letting the president convene "military commissions" at his discretion to try anyone he designates an "unprivileged enemy belligerent," with the right to detain them indefinitely in secret;

• providing only cursory and speedy trials or none at all;

• letting torture-coerced confessions be used as evidence in trial proceedings, despite US and international law prohibiting cruel and inhuman treatment at all times, under all conditions, with no allowed exceptions;

• letting hearsay and secret evidence be used; and

• denying due process and judicial fairness overall.

On the same October day in 2007, George Bush quietly signed the *National Defense Authorization Act* (NDAA). Included were hidden Sections 1076 and 333 which amended the 1807 *Insurrection Act* and 1878 *Posse Comitatus Act* prohibiting using federal and National Guard troops for domestic law enforcement except as constitutionally allowed or expressly authorized by Congress in times of insurrection or other national emergency.

Henceforth, the executive, by diktat, can claim emergency powers, declare martial law, suspend the Constitution on "national security" grounds, and deploy federal and/or National Guard troops on US streets to suppress whatever it calls disorder, including lawful peaceful protests. At issue is the abolition of fundamental First Amendment freedoms without which all others are at risk, such as free expression, freedom of assembly, religion, and the right to petition government for redress.

On May 21, 2009, Obama addressed national security and civil liberties issues, including Guantanamo detainees, military commissions, and torture. Saying his "single most important responsibility as president is to keep the American people safe," he bogusly claimed Al Qaeda "is actively planning to attack us again [and] this threat will be with us for a long time...." He added that uncharged detainees "who cannot be prosecuted yet who pose a clear danger to the American people" [with or without evidence to prove it] will be held indefinitely without trial.

Obama's March 7, 2011 Executive Order authorized military commission trials for Guantanamo detainees with revamped procedures, despite his pledge to close the prison.

On December 5, 2011 the ACLU headlined, "Indefinite Detention, Endless Worldwide War and the 2012 National Defense Authorization Act (NDAA)," saying that the enactment of this measure authorizes "the military to pick up and imprison people, including US citizens, without charging them or putting them on trial."

Secretly, with no hearings, both Houses rushed to enact a "joint version" before leaving for Christmas break.

On December 13, the Center for Constitutional Rights (CCR) urged Obama to veto NDAA in its present form or he would "be responsible for signing into law one of the greatest expansions of executive power in our nation's history, allowing the government to lock up citizens and non-citizens without the right to fair trials."

Indefinite detentions without trial violate core democratic freedoms, including fundamental Bill of Rights freedoms dating back to 1791. When Franklin Roosevelt issued Proclamation 2524 in 1941, he declared December 15 as Bill of Rights Day, commemorating 150 years since its ratification.

At the time, he hailed "America['s] charter of personal liberty and human dignity," including "freedom of religion, freedom of speech, freedom of the press, freedom of assembly, and the free right to petition the Government for redress of grievances."

Although American freedom then was actually far less than he claimed, today it's vanishing in plain sight.

142

In response to global imperial wars, corporate favoritism, unbridled private sector criminality, and political corruption at the highest levels, causing economic crisis conditions at home, thousands began protesting nationwide for social justice. In response, militarized police confronted them violently as NDAA headed for enactment to be able to stop anyone from challenging US hegemony and corporate power by throwing them indefinitely in military dungeons to rot.

Equity and justice are disappearing in order to advance America's imperium. On May 26, 2011 the House passed HR 1540 by a vote of 322 to 96. This marked a giant step toward abolishing freedom entirely.

On December 1, 2011, the Senate's S. 1867 followed suit, passing near unanimously by a vote of 93 to 7. Both versions assure that now no one is safe anywhere, including law-abiding US citizens. In mid-December, Congress enacted a joint bill. After promising a veto, Obama signed it on December 31, a day that will live in infamy.

This means anyone anywhere, including US citizens, may be indefinitely held without charge or trial, based solely on suspicions, baseless allegations or without any grounds at all. No reasonable proof is required, just suspicions that those detained pose threats. Henceforth, indefinite detentions can result from mere membership (past or present) in or support for suspect organizations.

Presidents now have unchecked authority to arrest, interrogate and indefinitely detain law-abiding citizens if accused of potentially posing a threat. Constitutional, statute and international laws don't apply. Presidential diktats have replaced them. US military personnel are authorized to arrest and indefinitely detain anyone globally, including US citizens..

Senate bill sponsor Carl Levin said administration officialslobbied against language excluding US citizens from indefinite military detentions without trials or due process. According to Levin:

> The language which precluded the application of Section 1031 to American citizens was in the bill that we originally approved... and the administration asked us to remove [it] which says that US citizens and lawful residents would not be subject to this section.
>
> ... It was the administration which asked us to remove the very language, the absence of which is now objected to.

In other words, Obama has no objection to US citizens being indefinitely detained in military prisons whether or not charges are brought against them. He fully supports police state repression. Only his disingenuous rhetoric says otherwise. Earlier by Executive Order, he authorized indefinite detention of anyone designated as a national security threat. Specifically intended for Guantanamo detainees, this legislation has now been extended to include everyone, including US citizens at home or abroad.

Moreover, CIA operatives and Special Forces death squads received presidential authorization to kill targeted US citizens abroad. This means that US citizens can be hunted down and murdered in cold blood for any reason or none at all.

Outspoken Muslim cleric Anwar al-Awlaki, a US citizen living in Yemen at the time, was killed for opposing Washington's imperium, not for any committed or even alleged crimes. His murder comes perilously close to replicating targeted assassinations at home, whether covertly or openly. In fact, administration lawyers view US citizens as legitimate targets if deemed national security threats, with or without corroborating evidence. As a result, indeed no one's safe, with or without NDAA's passage.

According to CIA counsel Stephen Preston and Pentagon lawyer Jeh Johnson, US citizens who are deemed to be at war with America have no immunity. Executive branch officials, not courts, will decide guilt or innocence issues.

Inviolable rights no longer apply. Protesting imperial lawlessness, social injustice, corporate crime, government corruption, or political Washington run of, by and for rich elites can be criminalized. So can free speech, assembly, religion, or anything challenging America's right to kill, destroy and pillage with impunity.

Tyranny has officially arrived in America.

Watering Down NDAA?

On February 28, 2012 Obama signed a "Presidential Policy Directive—Requirements of the National Defense Authorization Act," stating that "The executive branch must utilize all elements of national power—including military, intelligence, law enforcement, diplomatic, and economic tools—to effectively confront" national security threats.

At the same time, he authorized executive waiver power to grant exemptions from NDAA's section 1022(a)(1). An accompanying Fact Sheet explained, saying:"Section 1022 does not apply to U.S. citizens, and the President has decided to waive its application to lawful permanent residents arrested in the United States."

To be exempt, US citizens must be "arrested in this country or arrested by a federal agency on the basis of conduct taking place in this country." So exemptions are possible, but these require case by case executive decisions; and NDAA Section 2022 still applies to US citizens arrested abroad. Moreover, debate continues on whether or not those at home should be arrested under the NDAA, and for what reasons.

Post-9/11, numerous police state laws were enacted. Constitutional protections either eroded or ended. Obama's Policy Directive softening NDAA looks more like electoral politics than any conviction of the need to soften what he, himself, lobbied for and enacted. As a result, US citizens may be as much at risk now as before his Directive.

What's Behind Abolishing Due Process Protections

Main Street Europe and America face protracted Depression conditions. As a result, millions have lost jobs, homes, incomes, and their futures. Human misery is growing. So is public anger, raging across America and Europe. Gerald Celente put it pointedly, saying: "When people lose everything and have nothing else to lose, they lose it."

These Draconian police state provisions have been enacted to contain them. Military dungeons or secret FEMA camps may await them. Martial law may authorize it, claiming "catastrophic emergency" powers. Senators blew their cover when they called America a "battleground."

During WW II, loyal Japanese Americans were lawlessly detained. Today, social justice protesters and others wanting change are at risk. Political Washington is targeting them to assure business as usual. Obama is fully on board.

Militaries exist to protect nations from foreign threats. The US Uniform Code of Military Justice (UCMJ) applies solely to its own personnel as authorized under the Constitution's Article I, Section 8, which states: "The Congress shall have Power... To make Rules for the Government and Regulation of the land and naval forces."

Now in America, while state and local police, the Justice Department and FBI are responsible for criminal investigations and prosecutions, on matters relating to alleged national security concerns, America's military may arrest and indefinitely detain anyone anywhere, including US citizens, based on suspicions, spurious allegations, or none at all, if presidents so order dictatorially.

Obama's Directive may, in fact, change nothing. George Washington University Law Professor Jonathan Turley expressed outrage, saying:

> I am not sure which is worse: the loss of core civil
> liberties or the almost mocking post hoc rationalization

for abandoning principle. The Congress and the President have now completed a law that would have horrified the Framers. Indefinite detention of citizens is something (they) were intimately familiar with and expressly sought to bar in the Bill of Rights.[1]

Other legal scholars agree about all alleged criminals having habeas, due process, and other legal rights in duly established civil courts. Military tribunals are constitutionally illegal. Since June 2004, America's (conservative) High Court has made three landmark rulings.

In *Rasul v. Bush* (June 2004), the Court granted Guantanamo detainees habeas rights to challenge their detentions in civil court. Congress responded with the 2005 Detainee Treatment Act (DTA), subverting the ruling.

In *Hamdan v. Rumsfeld*, the Supreme Court held that federal courts retain jurisdiction over habeas cases. It said Guantanamo Bay military commissions lack "the power to proceed because (their) structures and procedures violate both the Uniform Code of Military Justice and the four Geneva Conventions (of) 1949."

In October 2006, Congress responded a second time. As explained above, it enacted the Military Commissions Act (MCA) subverting the High Court ruling in a more extreme form. Undermining fundamental rule of law principles, it gave the administration extraordinary unconstitutional powers to detain, interrogate, torture and prosecute alleged terrorist suspects, enemy combatants, or anyone claimed to support them. It lets the President designate anyone anywhere in the world (including US citizens) an "unlawful enemy combatant" and empowers the President to arrest and detain them indefinitely in military prisons.

On June 12, 2008, the High Court again disagreed. In *Boumediene v. Bush*, it ruled that Guantanamo detainees retained habeas rights. MCA unconstitutionally subverts them. As a result, the administration has no legal authority to deny detainees due process in civil courts or to act as accuser, trial judge and executioner with no right of appeal or chance for judicial fairness.

Nonetheless, Section 2031 of the FY 2010 NDAA contained the 2009 Military Commissions Act (MCA). As explained above, the phrase "unprivileged enemy belligerent" replaced "unlawful enemy combatant." The language changed but not the intent to assume police state powers despite the efforts of the US Supreme Court itself to protect due process.

So far, military commissions haven't tried any Americans. But going forward, based on alleged national security concerns, they may under new draconian FY 2012 NDAA provisions.

Notably, Jose Padilla, a US citizen, was lawlessly held over three
and a half years in military and civilian confinement as an alleged "enemy
combatant." Charges against him were spurious. Yet he was denied due
process, tortured, brutalized, dehumanized, and transformed in solitary
confinement to mush.

Emotionally destroyed ahead of his civil trial, Padilla resembled,
his lawyer said, "a piece of furniture," unable to represent himself
properly in court. In military detention ahead of his court martial, Bradley
Manning's barbaric treatment may have left him less than fully able as well.

Lawlessness at Home and Abroad

Abroad, independent states are targeted to turn them into client
states. Tactics include threats, destabilization, violence, sanctions and war
if the other methods fail.

In 2011, Libya became NATO's latest charnel house. It was
ravaged and destroyed for profit. For months, Syria has been ruthlessly
targeted. Pressure's building for more. Anything ahead is possible,
including replicating the barbarism inflicted on Libya.

Iran's next. Washington's pushing the envelope aggressively. Its
tactics include provocations, subversion, fake accusations, assassinations,
attempted isolation, covert or direct confrontation, cyberwarfare, and
sanctions so punishing that they could well be regarded as acts of war.

In the past five years, four harsh rounds of sanctions were imposed
against Iran. In mid-December 2011, Congress enacted yet another, and
they're included in the FY 2012 NDAA. They're aimed at penalizing
foreign financial institutions doing business with Tehran's central bank,
its primary conduit for receiving oil revenues. US corporations, including
banks, are already prohibited from dealing with Iran. Additional measures
expanded the sanctions on companies doing oil-related business, including
making investments, selling Iran refinery goods and services, as well as
providing Tehran with refined products worth $5 million or more annually.

After signing NDAA, Obama has 180 days as at this writing to
implement it. He calls it the stiffest measure yet, saying: "Our intent is
to implement this law in a timed and phased approach so that we avoid
repercussions to the oil market and ensure that this damages Iran and
not the rest of the world." He has discretionary power to grant waivers,
provided they're in America's national interest. Energy analysts fear
enactment means disruptively higher oil prices. Others worry that
confrontation may follow rogue bullying.

Navy Commander Rear Admiral Habibollah Sayyari said Iran's
naval forces can readily block the Strait of Hormuz in response to hostile

Western actions. He spoke a day after Iranian Vice President Mohammad Reza Rahimi warned not a drop of oil would pass through the Strait if Iran's oil exports are sanctioned. If this happens, expect energy prices to skyrocket until normal flows resume. Also expect retaliation, perhaps including a direct US-Iranian confrontation.

Targeting Iran's nuclear program is a red herring. Tehran insists it's peaceful. Nothing proves otherwise. The most recent March 2011 US intelligence consensus agreed. It found no evidence of weapons development. The real agenda is regime change because of Iran's ongoing demonstrations of independence. Reasons are invented as pretext.

As a result, anything ahead is possible, including potentially devastating general war with nuclear weapons targeting underground Iranian facilities. No matter the risk, Obama seems headed for the unthinkable.

A Final Comment

For years, America has crept closer to totalitarian rule. Notably, the 1996 *Antiterrorism and Effective Death Penalty Act* eased surveillance and death penalty restrictions, eroded habeas protection, and smoothed the way for repressive measures to follow.

Post-9/11, they proliferated. Constitutional protections have been systematically eliminated. FY 2012 NDAA provisions destroy fundamental Bill of Rights protections, including Fifth and Fourteenth Amendment due process rights.

The Fifth Amendment says, "No person shall be held to answer for a capital, or otherwise infamous crime, unless on a presentment or indictment of a Grand Jury.."

Moreover, no one shall "be subject for the same offense to be twice put in jeopardy of life or limb....be compelled (to bear) witness against himself, nor be deprived of life, liberty, or property, without due process of law...."

The Fourteenth Amendment says, "All persons born or naturalized in the United States and subject to the jurisdiction thereof, are" US citizens. "No state shall make or enforce any law which shall abridge the privileges or immunities of (US) citizens... nor shall any state deprive any person of life, liberty, or property, without due process of law...."

Overall, America's Constitution protects against unreasonable, arbitrary, or capricious laws not based on rule of law principles. The Supreme Court rulings affirmed these Bill of Rights protections. In November 2008, Justice Anthony Kennedy sided with a majority ruling, saying:

After carefully considering the relevance of the 10 inviolable rights that comprise the ideological foundation on which our nation is built, the court finds that these basic freedoms remain important for the time being, and should not be overturned.

Until such time as it can be definitively proven that citizens no longer require the protections provided by the Bill of Rights, it shall remain the principal legal guidance for the United States of America.

Under Obama and the 112th Congress, inviolability no longer applies. America's no different from other totalitarian states. As a result, no one challenging state power is safe. Denouncing imperial lawlessness can be criminalized. So can defending right over wrong. Constitutional protections don't apply.

Even before 9/11, Washington had begun militarizing police forces nationwide. Sophisticated weapons and training have been provided to them, including military robots, drones, M-16 assault rifles, helicopters, armored vehicles, grenade launchers, and other weapons previously used only by military forces.

In 1997, the so-called 1033 Program (formerly the 1208 Program) let the Defense Secretary "transfer, without charge, excess US Department of Defense (DoD) personal property (supplies and equipment) to state and local law enforcement agencies (LEAs)." As a result, domestic enforcement has been supplied with land, air and sea vehicles, weapons, computer equipment, body armor, fingerprint equipment, night vision equipment, radios and televisions, first aid equipment, tents, sleeping bags, photographic equipment, and more.

In 2011 alone, about $500 million in military related hardware was supplied. Next year's amounts are expected to increase fourfold. Doing so coincides with Occupation Wall Street crackdowns. More than ever, America's been militarized in preparation for quashing social justice protests at a time when equity and justice for the vast majority of Americans are disappearing. Moreover, military forces may be called upon to intervene if local cops need help.

They're coming for anyone challenging injustice, and when they do, there's no rule of law to turn. Constitutional, statute, and international law protections no longer apply. Tyranny has been legislated in. Only people power can set things right.

ENDNOTES

1   <http://shiftfrequency.com/jonathan-turley-obama-broke-his-promise/>

23

BANKER
OCCUPATION
OF GREECE

Back in June, 2011, economist Michael Hudson put the breaking situation in Greece in a nutshell. In an article titled "How Financial Oligarchy Replaces Democracy,"[1] he pointed out how, after being debt entrapped, or perhaps acquiescing to entrapment, the (then) Papandreou government needed bailout help to pay bankers that entrapped them. Doing so, however, required that the government initiate a class war by raising its taxes (on working households), lowering [their] standard of living—and even private-sector pensions—and selling off public land, tourist sites, islands, ports, water and sewer facilities."

Virtually everything since then has gone up for sale—all the country's crown jewels, lock, stock and barrel. Investor predators are strip-mining them of everything of worth at fire sale prices. That's how predatory capitalism works. The US-dominated IMF, EU and European Central Bank (ECB), the so-called "Troika," demanded it as the price for bailout help. It wouldn't be needed if Greece wasn't trapped in the euro straightjacket.

Membership in the European Union requires that a country maintain sovereignty over its money to monetize its debt freely, foregoing the right to devalue its currency to make exports more competitive, and the ability to legislate fiscal policies to stimulate growth. Instead they're vulnerable to entrapment by foreign banker diktats demanding tribute. The situation in Greece was and is called a "rescue." In fact, it's Troika-enforced plunder.

In May 2010, the Papandreou government agreed to austerity in return for loans. Then successive governments agreed to more of both.

Whatever financial oligarchs want, they get. In Greece and across Europe, people's needs go begging.

What's ongoing is government sanctioned financial coup d'etat. Former Wall Street broker, financial analyst and radio/TV host Max Keiser calls it "banker occupation" for good reason. They:

- make the rules;

- set the terms;

- issue diktats;

- pressure, bribe or otherwise cajole or force governments to acquiesce; and

- burden working households with higher unemployment, wage and benefit cuts, higher taxes, and other austerity measures to assure financial predators profit.

Once prosperous nations are surrendering their sovereignty to bailouts that only enrich bankers. Predatory money power rules the world.

Hudson pointed out how European central planning concentrated financial power in "non-democratic hands" from its inception under European Central Bank (ECB) dominance. Operating like a financial czar over its 17 Eurozone members, it "has no elected government [to] levy taxes" while "[t]he EU constitution prevents [it] from bailing out governments," unlike the Fed, which is able to monetize US debt in limitless amounts. Furthermore, "the IMF Articles of Agreement also block it from giving domestic fiscal support for budget deficits":

> A member state may obtain IMF credits only on the condition that it has 'a need to make the purchase because of its balance of payments or its reserve position or developments in its reserves.'

However, despite ample foreign exchange reserves, IMF loans are offered "because of budgetary problems," precisely what it's not allowed to do. As a result, "when it comes to bailing out bankers," said Hudson, "rules are ignored" to save them and their counterparties from incurring losses. And it works the same way in America under the Fed. Open-checkbook amounts are handed to Wall Street on demand.

Hudson calls finance "a form of warfare." It operates like pillaging armies. It takes over land, infrastructure, other tangible assets, and all material wealth. In the process, nations are devastated.

Unemployment, poverty neo-serfdom, demographic shrinkage, shortened life spans, emigration and capital flight follow.

Greece's business-friendly fiscal legacy caused today's crisis Financial deception followed. On February 8, 2010, *Der Spiegel* writer Beat Balzli headlined, "Greek Debt Crisis: How Goldman Sachs Helped Greece to Mask its True Debt,"[2] describing how in 2002, Goldman helped Greece borrow billions by circumventing Eurozone rules. Creative accounting hid Greek debt through off-balance sheet shenanigans. Derivatives were used, called "cross-currency swaps in which government debt issued in dollars and yen was swapped for euro debt for a certain period—to be exchanged back into the original currencies at a later date."

Greece's debt entrapment followed. In 2010, in return for a $150 billion loan, then Prime Minister Papandreou imposed:

- large public worker layoffs (around 10% overall);

- public sector 10% wage cuts, including a 30% reduction in salary entitlements;

- cuts to civil service bonuses of 20%;

- a freeze on pensions;

- a rise in the average retirement age by two years; and

- higher fuel, alcohol, tobacco, and luxury goods taxes.

Successive bailout help was needed and it still is. The more receoved, the greater Greek debt. It's heading the country in a downward cycle to oblivion. Previous austerity included

- laying off another 20% of public workers;

- privatizing public enterprises and assets, selling them off on the cheap;

- a one-time personal income levy from 1-5%, depending on income;

- lowering the tax-free income threshold to 8,000 euros annually from 12,000;

- setting the lowest tax rate at 10%, with exemptions for people up to age 30, over-65 pensioners, and disabled people; and

- annually taxing the self-employed an additional 300 euros.

Greece: Profile of a Failed State

Now, two years later, Greece exhibits failed and rogue state characteristics. It governs irresponsibly. It's beholden more to foreign interests than to its own. Banker needs are still prioritized. The ruling authority outside Greece dictates the terms. The country's unable or refuses to provide public services, threatening the welfare of its people. Governments have risen and fallen. Greece is bankrupt but won't declare it.

Governance in Greece combines travesty, tragedy and shame, as democracy's birth place spurns it. It displays an unprincipled disregard for human need at a time of rampant corruption and prioritized military spending. In 2011, seven billion euros went for arms to fulfill Greece's commitment to NATO, It's one of 28 NATO countries whose collective defense requires member states buy from alliance partners. Greece is the tenth largest weapons importer. As a percentage of GDP, Greek defense spending is nearly double that of other EU nations. Germany is one of Athens' main creditors. It's also one of its largest arms suppliers. Greece accounts for 15% of Berlin's weapons exports.

No justification for such spending exists, particularly in the midst of economic breakdown. Greece has no enemies. It's also broke. It can't or won't provide public services. It borrows hugely to repay and service debt, and rampant corruption is out of control.

Transparency International (TI) says

> Greek people live in a state of 'corrupt legality,' meaning that the law often condones or even fosters corrupt practices. Corruption is endemic: not limited to any party or social class, nor to the public sector.
>
> The public sector suffers from substantial gaps in both law and practice, thus allowing corruption to thrive. Public officials have been allowed to act for decades without any transparency or effective oversight.
>
> As a result, lack of integrity, tendency to demand and accept bribes, and unfaithfulness to public service have proliferated. Wrongdoing has eroded the rule of law and facilitated a culture of impunity.[3]

Privileged elites hide their wealth in favored tax havens. Capital flight explains part of Greece's problem. This unaccountability lets them get away with what no one should tolerate. It's especially outrageous at a time of economic crisis and appalling human deprivation. Force-feeding more pain exacerbates deplorable conditions.

Last May, 2012, the dominant parties polled poorly. Voters rejected austerity. Many voted with their feet and opted out. Ordinary Greeks are beset by crushing wage, benefit, and other social cuts. Impoverishment, homelessness, and unemployment were the result. Public anger expresses itself in street protests, strikes, and a search for opportunities elsewhere. Some of Greece's best and brightest are leaving. Why stay without job prospects or futures? Other professionals abroad aren't returning.

Dire economic conditions are creating a lost generation. The brain drain exodus affects the country's future. Greece is inhospitable to human welfare. Who can survive without jobs, income or futures?

Rage against rogue governance grows. On November 6, 2012, *The New York Times* headlined "Normal Life on Pause, and a Sense of Simmering Rage," saying that proprietors are going out of business for lack of enough customers and revenue to cover expenses. Deepening Depression conditions exist. Greece's economy is on a downward spiral to oblivion.

> The vitriol toward politicians is in many ways more intense than the outrage expressed toward the European Union and the International Monetary Fund.
>
> Politicians here rarely venture out in public, and when they do, even the most obscure member of Parliament is accompanied by at least one bodyguard.[4]

On November 7, more austerity measures were enacted, some of the most draconian so far. Street rage became violent. Prior to the vote, 100,000 angry Greeks marched on parliament in Syntagma Square. Why they haven't stormed it so far, they'll have to explain. Don't be surprised if they do in future, in a country best described as a tinderbox ready to explode. People only take so much. Once the pain levels exceed a threshold of no return, all bets are off. Politicians are playing with fire. Revolutionary anger is visceral. One spark too many may ignite it.

Police used tear gas and water cannons to disperse crowds. Protesters threw Molotov cocktails at security forces. A bus stop and kiosk were set ablaze. Dozens of arrests followed. The arrest of hundreds or thousands more won't quell the rage. Greeks are justifiably mad and show it. It's perhaps just a matter of time before the whole country explodes.

The strikes brought Greece to a halt. Hospitals operated with skeleton crews. Commerce shut down. Journalists walked out. They joined strikers. Broadcasts and publications were suspended.

The Troika demanded and got another $17.2 billion in budget cuts. At issue is qualifying for $39.6 billion in bailout funds. Greece barely gets enough to pay the bureaucrats. Debt service and bailing out bankers get top priority. The term bailout is a misnomer anyway. Grand theft and extortion more accurately explain the policy victimizing ordinary Greeks and the Greek economy. The latter is a shell of its former self, a zombie waiting for its obituary to be written.

Prime Minister Antonis Samaris heads Greece's current rogue government. On November 7th, he said that Athens took "a big, decisive and optimistic step. A step toward recovery. I am very pleased." But the more Greece borrows, the greater its debt, the harder it is to service and repay, the more future aid that's needed, and faster the country heads toward total collapse.

Soon, more than buildings may burn. Politicians may be targeted. They could be tarred, feathered or shot. University of the Aegean lecturer Panagiotis Sotiris told Russia Today: "Every austerity package in the last two and a half years was supposed to be the last one. So it won't be the last one this time. We are going to see more of this."[5] With minimal discussion, parliament "pass[ed] a huge law. We are very far from democratic procedure. This is a set of measures, which are actually dictated by the Troika."

Ordinary Greeks have no say. Parliament has surrendered to diktat authority. A banner one protestor held expressed mass sentiment, saying: "TRAITOR SAMARAS GET OUT".

In August, Greek unemployment hit a record high. It's officially at 25.4%, which means that one in four workers have no jobs. Figures rose monthly for the last three years . The true rate of unemployment may be much higher. Moreover, most jobs pay subsistence wages and poor or no benefits. Young people are hardest hit. In the 15-24 age category, 58% are jobless. It's likely closer to two-thirds. In the last three years, wages have been cut up to 60%. Around 70,000 small businesses have ceased operating.

The latest austerity round targets another 150,000 jobs, further wage cuts up to 30%, pension cuts up to 15%, and fewer healthcare benefits. Bureaucrats across the board are affected. Minimum wages, holiday benefits, and severance pay will be reduced. Education will also be hit hard. Universities will be shut. Mass staff reductions will follow. The retirement age will be raised from 65 to 67. Job protections are weakened, with layoffs now easier. Redundancy notice was decreased from six to four months.

The done deal isn't quite complete. On November 11, 2011

parliamentarians will meet Troika officials. Their revised budget must be approved. Greece also wants more. It seeks a further "emergency growth package" worth another 10 billion euros. It's nowhere near enough for what Athens needs.

On November 5, Greek journalists walked out for the second time in a week. They're protesting plans to merge their social security fund with a national system. Finance Minister Yannis Stournaras initially couldn't get a parliamentary agreement to merge the social security funds of journalists, civil engineers, lawyers, and others into the National Organization for Healthcare Provisions (EOPYY). On November 7, the measure passed.

Greece stands at the abyss of collapse. It's mired in deepening Depression. Since 2007, its economy shrunk nearly 22% and continues heading south. Ordinary Greeks bear the greatest burden. Multiple rounds of wage cuts, layoffs and lost benefits created unforgivable hardships.

Bad as things are now, more force-fed austerity is planned. Expect no end of it ahead. Greece is banker occupied. It's debt entrapped. Class war rages as living standards plummet precipitously. Troika authorities demand a sell-off of state-run enterprises, public land, tourist sites, ports, water, and other Greek crown jewels stripped of all worth and sold at fire sale prices. Financial warfare is more destructive than pillaging armies.

Earlier hard times produced Nazism. World War II followed. Failure to learn from history risks repeating it. No one seems to notice or care. It may be too late to matter once reality hits home. And that may come sooner than most imagine. The neo-fascist Golden Dawn in Greece is arising.

ENDNOTES

1   <http://michael-hudson.com/2011/06/how-financial-oligarchy-replaces-democracy/>

2   <http://www.spiegel.de/international/europe/greek-debt-crisis-how-goldman-sachs-helped-greece-to-mask-its-true-debt-a-676634.html>

3   <http://issuu.com/transparencyinternational/docs/2012_nis_greece_en?mode=window&backgroundColor=%23222222>

4   <http://www.nytimes.com/2011/11/07/world/europe/in-greece-economic-crisis-brings-rage-and-paralysis.html?_r=1&>

5   <http://rt.com/news/greece-austerity-bill-protests-144/>

24

RESPONSIBLE
NEW YORK
BANKING

Founded in 1882, the Bank of Cattaraugus (B of C) exception proves the rule. Located in Western New York, it's miles from Wall Street's cesspool of fraud, market manipulation, grand theft, bailouts, and influence peddling with corrupt politicians who are getting generous campaign contribution bribes in return.

B of C calls itself "one of the oldest and strongest banks in New York state... a full-service, independent bank that provides financial services with a hometown touch. Personal, friendly service is our signature trademark, and we're dedicated to give back to the communities we service."

B of C "operate[s] with the same belief that the needs of the local community and its residents are its business. Local deposits must remain available for local loans to sustain" Cattaraugus village, located about an hour south of Buffalo.

Imagine a bank anywhere operating honestly and responsibly, meaning what it says, and proving it. Grateful B of C customers say so. More on that below.

With about $16 million in assets and $1.1 million in equity capital, B of C is microbank in size, well below the $10 billion small bank ceiling. Its business model stresses serving local community needs. About 80% of its loans involve mortgages to local residents.

It's the state's smallest bank with one location and eight employees. It's Cattaraugus' only bank.

B of C doesn't base loans on credit scores. Knowing community needs well, it operates supportively to help. In its history, annual profits rarely exceeded $50,000. In 2010, it earned $47,000 for a 0.3% return on assets. Despite its size and low profitability, President and CEO Patrick

Cullen says twice weekly, on average, larger banks make buyout offers. No thanks, he responds. "There's nothing they can offer us that we can't do ourselves." He prefers independence, sticking with his simple business model, operating like a public utility, avoiding high risks, reinvesting in Cattaraugus' economy, and helping local residents.

B of C doesn't operate parasitically. It doesn't speculate in financial derivatives and an alphabet soup of securitized garbage. It won't cheat customers, make liar's loans, bilk investors through fraudulent schemes, or engage in other manipulative, dishonest practices. It hasworked for 130 years as the only bank in a community of about 1,000 residents. Operating privately, it replicates responsible public banking.

On December 23, *New York Times* writer Alan Feuer's article, "The Bank Around the Corner,"[1] cited pensioner Carol Bonner, one of many grateful B of C customers, who needed a loan for car repairs. Cullen helped her as he had done, earlier. "A few years ago, when [she] fell behind on her property taxes and was forced to sell her home, Cullen (as mortgage holder) had his son Thomas (a Chicago resident) buy it." As a result, Bonner and her sister stayed as renters.

"The whole thing was incredible," Bonner said. "I just didn't realize there were people like that in the world who would help you. Especially a banker."

B of C is different. It holds village deposits and "lend[s] to its neediest inhabitants." Recently it granted forbearance to an unemployed bus mechanic mortgagee. Another Amish customer needed $85,000 for debt consolidation. Despite earning only $2,300 a year selling greenhouse starter kits, he got it. According to Cullen, "If you know Amish culture, you know his sons work and that everything they earn goes to him until they're 21 or married. So he was fine, but none of that shows up on a credit score."

Diner owner Paul Macakanja says, "They do things that big banks won't do. They support you personally because your success is their success."

Through responsible lending to local community residents and businesses, stressing customer service, offering access to management, and understanding borrower needs well, bottom line concerns are served sustainably long-term.

"If it sounds old-fashioned, it is," said *Times* reporter Feuer. "It's not the kind of bank you'll find anymore in New York City" or other large communities.

Retired worker Duane Kelley said, "They saved our lives" after he lost his home over a $15,000 tax lien. Cullen bought the house with bank money, returned it to Kelly, and he's repaying B of C through a 15-year loan.

Bank examiners ask Cullen, "When are you going to grow?" He responds saying, "But where is it written I have to grow? We take care of our customers. The truth is we probably couldn't grow too much in a town like this."

Cattaraugus has limited prospects. Except for a lollipop handle producer, its former manufacturing base died. Its largest employer is the school district, "and many village residents survive... on pensions or government subsidies, in homes" with average $30,000 mortgages.

B of C is a family business. Cullen's daughter is chief financial officer and wife Joan corporate secretary. With giant banks bigger than ever during hard times and historically low interest rates, small banks are hard-pressed to compete. Yet growing anger over banking fraud, predatory lending, high fees, and lack of public service encourages depositors to move funds to smaller, local institutions.

The Move Your Money project[2] encourages the movement to smaller banks, telling people to vote with their dollars, "Invest in Main Street, Not Wall Street." So does Bank Transfer Day.org.[3] Inspired by OWS, it encourages credit union banking. According to organizer Kristen Christian:

> I started this because I felt like many of you do. I was tired—tired of the fee increases, tired of not being able to access my money when I need to, tired of them using what little money I have to oppress my brothers and sisters...
>
> So I stood up. I've been shocked at how many people have stood up alongside me. With each person who RSVPs to this event, my heart swells. [With] each of YOU standing with me....they can't drown out the noise we'll make

Christian claims she persuaded 400,000 people to shift from large banks to not-for-profit credit unions.

In today's environment, Independent Community Bankers of America (ICBA)[4] president Camden Fine believes small banks are especially important. They hold 20% of banking assets and write over half of small business loans. According to Fine, "Customers can say, 'I know where my money is—it's down there eight blocks away. They can walk in and talk to the president and know he isn't sucking in their money and betting against them on proprietary securities."

Cullen believes rural banking is vital. Moreover, "(w)hen customers entrust their life savings to us, we treat them as if it were our own." Among other projects, he bought an old town hotel. He's waiting for a chance to use it. He also plans restoring original town buildings. He hopes to open them as a colonial Williamsburg-style theme park. "If you look at Williamsburg's web site," he says, "they claim the park employs 3,800 people. Give us 5% of that, I'll claim success." It will be entirely home grown. "Everyone will be involved. The bank, the church, local government, the people—everyone will have a stake." It's what it's all about.

Nonetheless, since 2008, hundreds of community banks have gone under.

Public Banking: An Idea Whose Time Has Come

Establishing *public banks that operate like B of C* across America is vital at a time of financialized power, casino capitalism, depression-sized unemployment, socialized losses, privatized profits, and Wall Street crooks operating an unprecedented money making racket. This can be done by working cooperatively with responsible community banks like B of C and non-profit credit unions—with the added depositors' security factor that public banks are based on the creditworthiness of the state, community or federal government.

Like B of C, public banks provide low-interest loans to businesses, farmers, communities, households, students, and other worthy borrowers as a way to revive and sustain inflation-free prosperity. They don't have to earn profits. They're not beholden to Wall Street or shareholders.

It's no pipe dream. It's real. It happened before. It's happening in North Dakota, the only state with a publicly owned bank, and can anywhere they're established.

So far, in over 230 years, no state ever went out of business, and, except for Arkansas during the Great Depression, none ever defaulted, even when poorly governed.

Moreover, public banks can lend to themselves and to municipalities interest-free, as well as to businesses, farmers, and individuals at low affordable rates to create sustainable, inflation-free growth. Notably, the more often loans roll over, the more debt-free money is created—inflation-free if used productively for growth, not speculation, big bonuses and other excesses—as would be the case. In fact, as long as new money produces goods and services, inflation can't occur. Only imbalances cause problems when demand exceeds supply. In contrast, price stability is assured when both increase proportionally.

It's not pie-in-the-sky. It works and can return money power to public hands where it belongs. Establishing a system of public banking will end Wall Street's ability to commit massive fraud and create asset bubbles, record budget and national debt levels, depression-sized unemployment, human need and anger.

Today's financial contagion is global. Billions suffer. Economies are being wrecked to save the banks. Washington is Wall Street-occupied territory. So are the European financial capitals as governments provide trillions of dollars to socialize losses, privatize profits, and hang their own citizens out to dry.

Replacing a predatory system with public banks working responsibly with small communities—ones like B of C and non-profit credit unions—can change things.

Now is the time to build a just and equitable system. Besides peace, good will, democratic values, and government, of, by, and for everyone, what better idea is there than that? It's needed more than ever!

ENDNOTES

1 < http://www.nytimes.com/2011/12/25/nyregion/the-bank-of-cattaraugus-new-york-states-smallest-bank-plays-an-outsize-role. html?pagewanted=1&_r=2&hp>
2 < http://www.facebook.com/MoveYourMoney>
3 < http://www.facebook.com/Nov.Fifth>
4 < http://www.icba.org/>

25

PUBLIC BANKING WORKS

Publicly-owned banks work as intended. Colonial America had them for 25 years. Tax and inflation-free prosperity followed. The money that was created produced economic growth. It ended when Bank of England scoundrels regained control of money creation.

Public banks aren't predatory profiteers. They're not beholden to Wall Street, shareholders, or greedy corporate executives. They serve communities, states or nations responsibly. It works the same way everywhere they exist.

North Dakota is America's only public banking state. Established in 1919, it's 100% state owned. It partners responsibly with private banks. As a result of its public banking, North Dakota experiences growth instead of being forced to cut back like other states. It passes on the benefits to residents.

North Dakota has the nation's lowest unemployment rate. In September 2012, the Bureau of Labor Statistics ranked it number one at 3.0%. During the height of the 2008 economic crisis, North Dakota had its largest budget surplus in state history. Benefits were shared with residents.

While other states are struggling to manage, North Dakota alone prospers. Imagine if all states were run the same way. Hiring instead of firing would be policy. Economic hardships would be minimized or avoided. Federal, state and local debt could be substantially reduced or eliminated. Taxes could be minimized. Economic growth would be prioritized. So would job creation. Social programs could be funded inflation-free. Universal healthcare and education to the highest levels would be possible. Home foreclosures would end. Everyone would have access to low interest rate loans. Vital infrastructure could be rebuilt and protected against disasters like Hurricane Sandy. Booms and busts would end. Ordinary people would be helped just like rich ones are now. Private pensions, savings, and investments would be secure.

Ellen Brown heads the Public Banking Institute (PBI). It's an idea whose time has come. You should check it out at http://publicbankinginstitute.org/home.htm. Public banks differ from private ones. They're mandated to serve the public interest. They're not beholden to shareholders and corporate executives. Profits and personal gain aren't prioritized. In 1997, the Bank of North Dakota (BND) saved Grand Forks. It acted responsibly after massive Red River flooding. More on that below.

Imagine if New York, New Jersey, and other Sandy Hurricane-affected states had North Dakota's public banking advantage now. Struggling to recover from Hurricane Sandy would be much easier. Help where it's most needed is spotty. For over a week afterward, millions in New York, New Jersey, and other states still lacked electricity. The Bayonne NJ 16 million barrel International Matex Tank Terminal was closed for days. The pipeline servicing it was down, unable to operate without power.

Public transportation was impacted. Portions of New York's subway were flooded. Service was spotty for days. People couldn't get to work. Fuel was in short supply, and rationing was imposed. While most of Lower Manhattan had power five days later, outer boroughs and New Jersey weren't as fortunate And had to wait another week or longer. The Brooklyn-Battery Tunnel and others were flooded.

Waters surrounding New York City have been rising an inch a decade. The pace is increasing. Nothing is done to stop it. Infrastructure needs aren't prioritized. When downtown Chicago flooded in 1992, it took two weeks to remove water and nine months of additional work to repair damage and return things to normal. Sandy's destruction is far more extensive. Many area residents can expect protracted hardships.

Fuel oil distributors weren't sure when shipments would resume normally. As temperatures drop, working class communities have no heat. Many schools closed. Classes couldn't resume for over 100,000 New York City children for nearly two weeks at the earliest. Some schools may close permanently. In some areas, food and water were scarce. Many lost phone and Internet service. Public anger reacted to local, state and federal government incompetence, indifference, and the widespread failure to provide adequate relief.

Ordinary people are hardest hit. In two days, Wall Street was operating normally. It was prioritized, as were businesses and well-off areas. Throughout the crisis, working class areas got short shrift. Hospitals in poor communities suspended services for lack of power. City authorities didn't help.

Compare this to what happened in 1997, when Grand Forks was recovering from Red River floodingand had North Dakota's public banking at its back. . On November 3, 2012, the *Sky Valley Chronicle* headlined "Hurricane Sandy and the Great Red River Flood: How the Public Bank of North Dakota saved Grand Forks." Residents won't ever forget how in April 1997, the *Chronicle* wrote, record flooding and major fires devastated Grand Forks, ND. "They also won't forget that it was the Bank of North Dakota....that put people above profits."

BND rushed to help. Major Pat Owens ordered Grand Forks' largest evacuation since 1826. Around 50,000 residents were affected. Their troubles were just beginning. Emergency workers were hard-pressed to deal with flooding, power outages, destruction, and fires. Eleven buildings, 60 apartments, and the *Grand Forks Herald* were destroyed. Hundreds of other businesses were affected. Around 75% of area homes were damaged. Incredibly, not a single persom ... died ... But the town and its sister city, East Grand Forks (MN) lay in ruins." Floodwaters took two weeks to recede. "Property losses topped $3.5 billion." Homes, businesses, schools, and other buildings were affected. Some were damaged. Others were totally destroyed.

Straightaway, BND acted. It "began taking unprecedented [measures] to help families and businesses recover." A nearly $70 million credit line was established as follows:

- · "$15 million for the ND Division of Emergency Management

- · $10 million for the ND National Guard

- · $25 million for the City of Grand Forks

- · $12 million for the University of North Dakota, located in Grand Forks

- · $7 million allocated to raise the height of a dike at Devil's Lake, about 90 miles west of Grand Forks"

- Disaster loan relief was also offered. Around $5 million was allocated to help areas recover.

"BND led the way in getting people back on their feet." It responded proactively. Local financial institutions allocated matching funds. Millions of dollars went for recovery.

BND coordinated with the US Department of Education to ensure forbearance on student loans.» It «also worked closely with the Federal Housing Administration and Veterans Administration to gain forbearance on federally backed home loans and to establish a center where people could apply for federal/state housing assistance.

BND coordinated disaster fund relief with the North Dakota Community Foundation. It lowered interest rates on «Family Farm and Farm Operating programs» helping them to restructure debt and speed recovery.It arranged low interest rate Federal Home Loan Bank funding and passed on benefits to flood-affected borrowers.

From April 1997-2000, Grand Forks lost 3% of its population. East Grand Forks, Minnesota fared much worse. It lost 17% over the same time frame. While Grand Forks residents experienced public banking benefits firsthand when they most needed them, sister city EGF had no such advantage. Nor did flood-ravaged post-Katrina New Orleans.

New York, New Jersey, and other impacted states today are similarly disadvantaged. Multiple woes hamper them. Sandy compounded them. Imagine the difference if they had public banks to help.

Viable day-to-day and crisis solutions would help ordinary people, communities, businesses, and other institutions. Recovery efforts for troubled areas would begin straightaway. No one would be left out. Services would be provided for everyone needing them. Profiteering isn›t in public banking›s vocabulary. North Dakotans are served responsibly. Grand Forks residents know it best of all.

A Final Comment

On Sunday, New York Mayor Michael Bloomberg and Governor Andrew Cuomo compared Sandy to post-Katrina New Orleans. Both officials cited a "massive public housing problem." Up to 40,000 residents need new homes, they said. It was hard to tell precisely what they meant since affordable housing has been in crisis for years.

Since the 1980s, low-income housing assistance has been significantly cut. By the 1990s, hundreds of thousands of public housing units were dilapidated. Many were demolished and not replaced. Federal funding dropped precipitously. States and cities did little on their own.

Upscale development is prioritized. Wealth is distributed up the food chain, not down. Ordinary people and America's poor increasingly are on their own.

Affordable public housing is badly needed, but it's disappearing. Chicago's Cabrini Green is instructive. When completed in 1962, it had 3,114 units for 15,000 people. By spring 2010, it was mostly demolished and by December, it was gone. The last of its residents were evicted.

This is happening across America. Upscale developments replace affordable housing. Homelessness grows as a result. Disaster capitalism exploits opportunities like weather-related events, but there's not much by way of profit in building affordable housing.

Free market triumphalism profits at the expense of social justice. Blank became beautiful in post-Katrina New Orleans as city Blacks were forced out of communities. What city officials couldn't do on their own, nature did for them. Many Blacks never returned. Upscale projects replaced them. Milton Friedman once said only crisis conditions produce real change. When they occur, capitalizing on opportunities follows.

Will Hurricane Sandy-affected residents suffer the same fate as New Orleans Blacks? Bloomberg, Cuomo, and other area officials left unsaid what may be planned. Profiteering from misery is longstanding policy. North Dakota's BND helped ordinary people rebuild. Northeast states have no public banks.

Instead of helping residents in need, officials may exploit them for profit. Crisis conditions present opportunities not available other times. You can expect the worst ahead. It's happened so often before.

26

FRANKLIN ROOSEVELT'S SECOND BILL OF RIGHTS

Ferdinand Lundberg's *Cracks in the Constitution* deconstructed what the framers had really created. He equated them with a Wall Street crowd, given their economic status and prominence as bankers, merchants, lawyers, politicians, judges, and overall wheeler-dealers. In 1787, they convened the Constitutional Convention for their own interests, not the general welfare as most people believe. It included the Bill of Rights protections—added belatedly, and not for reasons commonly believed. They were for the protection of property owners, who wanted:

   • free speech, press, religion, assembly and petition rights—for their own interests, not for those of "The People;"

   • due process of law and speedy public trials for themselves, if charged;

   • prohibition of quartering troops in their homes or on their land;

   • protection from unreasonable searches and seizures;

   • the right to have state militias protect them;

   • the right to bear arms, but not the way the 2nd Amendment today is interpreted; and

   • various other rights—for themselves. As privileged elites, they lied, connived, misinterpreted, misrepresented, and pretty much operated as they wished for their own self-interest, law or no law.

Yet, the Constitution is hailed as the "supreme law of the land," including its 27 Amendments. The last amendment, proposed on September 25, 1789, wasn't enacted until May 7, 1992. It prevented congressional salaries from taking effect until the beginning of the next term.

Franklin Roosevelt's Proposed Economic Bill of Rights

In 1933, in his first inaugural address, Roosevelt criticized Wall Street greed, saying: "They only know the rules of a generation of self-seekers. They have no vision, and where there is no vision the people perish."

On January 11, 1944, in his last State of the Union Address, Roosevelt proposed a second bill of rights. He said:

> This Republic had its beginning, and grew to its present strength, under the protection of certain inalienable political rights ... They were our rights to life and liberty.
>
> As our nation has grown in size and stature, however—-as our industrial economy expanded—-these political rights proved inadequate to assure us equality in the pursuit of happiness.

His solution was an "economic bill of rights," guaranteeing:

• employment with a living wage;

• freedom from unfair competition and monopolies;

• housing;

• medical care;

• education; and

• social security.

The 1935 Act was inadequate even though it kept millions of retirees, disabled, and qualified survivors from the ravages of poverty.

Today, these benefits are fast eroding. Obama administration neoliberal ideologues want social benefits slashed, then privatized en route to eliminating them altogether. What Roosevelt proposed but couldn't implement, political Washington wants to deny and take away cleverly so most people won't notice until it's too late to matter.

With WW II nearly won, Roosevelt stressed focusing the nation's energies and resources on finishing it. Among other measures, he suggested:

• "A realistic tax law—which will tax all unreasonable profit," corporate and individual;

• "A cost of food law" with floor and ceiling limits on prices; and

• reenactment of the October 1942 stabilization statute, pertaining to prices, wages and salaries, affecting the cost of living.

He continued saying:

> We have come to a clear realization of the fact that true individual freedom cannot exist without economic security and independence. Necessitous men are not free men. People who are hungry and out of a job are the stuff of which dictatorships are made.
>
> In our day these economic truths have become accepted as self-evident. We have accepted, so to speak, a second Bill of Rights under which a new basis of security can be established for all—regardless of station, race, or creed.

He then listed what he meant, covering:

• Opportunity.

• The right to a useful and remunerative job.

• The right to a good education.

• The right of every businessman, large and small, to trade in an atmosphere of freedom from unfair competition and domination by monopolies.

• Security.

• The right to adequate protection from the economic fears of old age, sickness, accident and unemployment.

- The right to adequate medical care and the opportunity to achieve and enjoy good health.

- The right of every family to a decent home.

- The right to earn enough to provide adequate food and clothing and recreation.

Partly implemented at best, they were positive recommendations. They have been the mirror opposite to policies enacted under both parties since the 1980s. Obama's imposed austerity is especially onerous at a time when stimulus is desperately needed.

For example, the 1944 *Servicemen's Readjustment Act* (the GI Bill) provided college or vocational education for 7.8 million returning vets plus a year of unemployment compensation. In addition, 2.4 million got VA-backed low-interest, no down payment home loans at a time their average cost was under $5,000. It enabled millions of families to afford homes, many with government help. Later studies showed the GI Bill paid for itself sevenfold. It's considered one of America's best ever investments.

Roosevelt called his proposal "security. And after this war is won we must be prepared to move forward, in the implementation of these happiness and well-being" measures in the interest of democracy, humanity, fairness, justice, and a nation discharging its responsibilities for all its citizens equitably.

Today, these ideas are lost. At a time of an unprecedented wealth gap, officials ignore the essential needs of growing millions of ordinary people. They're on their own and out of luck because America's duopoly spurns them.

Instead, government priorities include imperial wars, handouts to bankers and other corporate favorites, and repressive laws. They're eroding freedoms, destroying them incrementally or entirely. Banana republic domination and exploitation replaces them.

FDR's prescription was different. Even though he was a patricianand gave back to save capitalism, his policies reflected the time's needs. It was the opposite of today's destructive response which is bankrupting the nation and making it not fit to live in.

It doesn't have to be that way and shouldn't be. America could grow again productively and serve everyone. Higher taxes and federal debt aren't needed to accomplish it. Giving people money power back can do it, inflation free.

Henry Ford once said:

It is well enough that the people of the nation do not understand our banking and monetary system, for if they did, I believe there would be a revolution before tomorrow morning.

www.ingramcontent.com/pod-product-compliance
Lightning Source LLC
Chambersburg PA
CBHW070249290326
41930CB00041B/2314